memoried and storied

memoried and storied

HEALING OUR SHARED HISTORY
OF **RACIAL VIOLENCE**

dr. judith reifsteck

TOP READS PUBLISHING, LLC

VISTA, CALIFORNIA

For information about permissions, and special discounts for bulk purchases, address: Top Reads Publishing Subsidiary Rights Department, 1035 E. Vista Way, Suite 205, Vista, CA 92084 USA, or email teri@topreadspublishing.com.

Names: Reifsteck, Judith, author.
Title: Memoried and storied : healing our shared history of racial violence / Dr. Judith Reifsteck.
Description: First edition. | Vista, California : Top Reads Publishing, LLC, [2023] | Includes
              bibliographical references and index.
Identifiers: ISBN: 978-1-970107-32-6 (hardcover) | 978-1-970107-33-3 (ebook) | LCCN: 2022914405
Subjects: LCSH: Harris, Charlotte--Death and burial. | Thompson, Allie--Death and burial. | James,
              John Henry--Death and burial. | Baker, Frazier--Death and burial. | Lynching--Southern
              States-- History. | African Americans--Violence against-Southern States--History. | African
              Americans--Crimes against-Southern States--History. | African Americans--Punishment
              & torture--Southern States--History. | African Americans--Southern States--Biography.
              | Southern States--Race relations-History. | Racism--Southern States. | Racism--United
              States. | Anti-lynching movements--United States. | United States--Race relations. |
              Memorialization --Southern States. | Memorialization--United States. | BISAC: SOCIAL
              SCIENCE / Ethnic Studies / American / African American & Black Studies. | BIOGRAPHY
              & AUTOBIOGRAPHY / Cultural, Ethnic & Regional / African American & Black. | SOCIAL
              SCIENCE / Race & Ethnic Relations.
Classification: LCC: HV6464 | DDC: 364.1/34--dc23

Cover design: Ann Weinstock
Front cover art credit: Ment Nelson, "Backwoods Baptism"
Back cover photo credit: Anne McQuary/The New York Times
Interior design: Caite Hamilton

See page 86 for complete list of image credits, used with permission.

For more information about the author visit: www.drjudithreifsteck.com

Printed in the United States of America

23 24 25 26 27   10 9 8 7 6 5 4 3 2 1

Dedication

For Ida B. Wells, Harriet Tubman, Ella Baker, Sojourner Truth, Diane Nash, Patrisse Cullors, Rosa Parks, Bryan Stevenson, Bree Newsome, Alicia Garza, Phillis Wheatley, Tarana Burke, Fannie Lou Hamer and so many others.

May we be wise enough to honor you.
May we have the courage to dream your dreams of freedom.
May we have the hope to teach others about those dreams.
May our faith move us to action so those dreams become our future.

Table of Contents

Prologue
Introduction

I became interested in writing a book about racial violence and shared healing after visiting the National Memorial for Peace and Justice. The memorial is a part of the Equal Justice Initiative, and it stands on a hillside overlooking the city of Montgomery, Alabama. On a peaceful, rolling green lawn adjacent to downtown, the visitor sees a massive collection of stone markers hanging from the ceiling of the beautifully designed space. The structure memorializes Black Americans lynched before, during, and after the period of Jim Crow legalized segregation in this country.

When you visit this national monument, it exposes you to our nation's history of White supremacy and the acts of racial terrorism it inspired. Before traveling to Montgomery, Alabama, in March 2021, I researched the documented known lynchings that had occurred in my own county and six adjacent counties. When I got there, I found the six-foot, heavy stone marker for each of our local victims hanging from the ceiling at the memorial site. The names on the coffins shared the space with 4,400 other names on 800 markers, one for every county in America where a lynching occurred.

Many people I respect suggested I share more with the reader about why I wrote a book about racial violence and what qualifies me to write about this topic. In 1999, when I wrote my dissertation on adolescents at risk for becoming perpetrators of antisocial acts and mass violence, I used the clinical and research skills learned in my doctoral training to do so. But my motivation for completing the current work, and the personal growth this project required, came not just from my research skills or an intellectual place but also from a different place. After progressing well into the center of the

"To see a place that was once considered a horror scene has now become a beautiful garden of **peace** and tranquility. It's not redemption, but it's something on that road."

—John Butler

writing, I realized that my intention this time came from my heart, my soul, my memories, and my own recovery journey. It came from the young child inside of me who had lived in a violent, alcoholic home as a small girl. When I first entered recovery, I was a married adult with three small children, and I desperately sought to break the cycle of parental violence against innocent kids that I had inherited. I had also married a survivor of family violence, and together, he and I were committed to applying what we were learning to our own young family.

Furthermore, this discovery of why I wrote this book was not as "accomplished," neat, and tidy as this description of the personal growth process would seem to imply. My experience is that none of this is easy. The work, whether it is organizing for racial equality or personally healing from being a victim of family violence, includes individual moments and long stretches of confronting your own limitations. In the case of the current book—although I may bring research skills and clinical experience that qualifies me to write about social problems or therapy for trauma healing—at the end of every day, I am still a White woman writing about the history of lynching in America. I seek to address that limitation by admitting what should be an obvious and crucial truth. I need leadership and help from Black collaborators and other people of color—help I have asked for and received. I am dedicated to racial equality activism and teaching about our nation's shameful history of racial terrorism. I am committed to ending the whitewashing and White amnesia of our historical narrative. I invite any reader or collaborator to check me when needed, tell me what I've missed or gotten wrong (because I will get things wrong), and help me get it right in my racial justice work and writing.

Many Americans are disconnected from ancestors and family members whom they long for and seek to find. My own genealogical search was to locate the mother I lost at birth, although the term genealogy is too cold and distant—in my opinion—when the relative is your mother. As a counseling practitioner and clinician and an individual who experienced separation from my birth parents, I know the grief and loss of the separated child. The experience impacts a person in deep and significant ways at every stage of development. This book tells the stories of lynchings. It has been discovered that two of the four people I write about were parents who were violently removed forever from their children's lives. Those children and their descendants are among the many relatives left behind and traumatized forever by these acts. I identify strongly with those children, and I'm moved to help others see them and identify with them.

Today as I write this book, through the grace of God and the fellowship of Alcoholics Anonymous, I am a recovering alcoholic with twenty-nine years of sobriety in AA. It was and is important for me to admit and amend the mistakes I made before entering recovery, as well as my ongoing mistakes, and to acknowledge my brokenness—to tell the truth about what, in my fear

A flag announcing a lynching is flown from the window of the NAACP headquarters on the street at 69 Fifth Ave., New York City. Beginning in 1920, the advocacy organization conducted public displays to amplify the systematic practice of racial violence.

PHOTO: LIBRARY OF CONGRESS

The Memorial for Peace and Justice in Montgomery, Alabama, is a beautiful and emotionally powerful memorial, spearheaded by Bryan Stevenson, founder of the Equal Justice Initiative.

and in my shame, I may want to hide from others. Because I personally received so much help when I was down, I know that standing in your truth works in the long run to solve a problem and recover from a broken past. I have learned in recovery that it is possible to share secrets and have a break with denial, the inevitable denial that all humans experience when struggling and facing hard truths.

Finally, a word on how this book has affected me personally. When I began to unlock the vault and share hidden American history with others, I found this:

1. More locked doors. And because I've never been able to resist the hunt to find what's hidden, I kept writing.

2. Several helpers with keys who want to go with me on the next search. I am richer for the journey.

3. In telling these stories, I discovered an even deeper commitment to pursuing antiracist education in combating discrimination and a more passionate desire to work with others to dismantle the White amnesia in our current historical narrative. Discrimination perpetrates more harm, and amnesia in the historical narrative supports racial divisiveness.

To tell the stories of Charlotte Harris, John Henry James, Allie Thompson, and Frazier Baker, I had to consult newspapers, historical archives, community members, and activists involved with the community remembrance project in all four regions I wrote about. This background research showed me there are countless numbers of loving, hardworking racial justice warriors who want to make deep healing work possible. As I stay involved, every day is a day that I feel the love and the light that emanates from that healing work, and this makes me feel that hope does exist for our broken country and for myself. If your next step is to contact these groups (listed in the appendix and discussed throughout the book) to begin to connect with them and help them achieve their mission, you will be participating in the healing of racial violence too.

Story

The Historical Narrative

History defines and informs our daily existence. The stories we tell, the memories we make, flow together like two distinct streams to form a river of common beliefs and feelings. Beneath our current political and social divide in America lies a story of unreconciled terror.

From 1870 to 1950, there were 100 documented lynchings in Virginia. Each of these represents an act of racial terror, social oppression, and systemic injustice. Virginia was not an exception. As a place, it was not even the worst in this gruesome category of extrajudicial violence and vigilante justice. Following the Civil War, organized groups used lynchings to turn back the gains made by formerly enslaved people following Emancipation and the passing of the Thirteenth Amendment. Researchers have documented 4,084 racial terror lynchings in twelve southern states between the end of Reconstruction in 1877 and 1950. Additionally, more than 300 racial terror lynchings occurred in other states during this time period. This book will tell the story of the dedicated efforts of researchers who have spent thousands of hours documenting terror lynchings in the twelve most active lynching states and in other states in America.

Speaking in the documentary *True Justice*, Equal Justice Initiative Director Bryan Stevenson states:

Thousands of people were dragged out of their homes, dragged through the streets, beaten, hung, burned, shot, and left for days to hang from a tree. In

"For in the end it is all about **memory**, its sources and its magnitude, and of course its consequences ...to forget the dead would be killing them a second time."

—Elie Wiesel

many cases, the sheriff would often post someone for days to make sure the body was there. Most times, these people were lynched for some social transgression. For breaking social norms. They were killed for breaking a social rule.[1]

Eventually, slavery ended, and sanctioned lynching as public spectacle stopped. While politicians and White supremacists set about overturning the gains of Reconstruction, a series of heroic efforts were put forth to advance the cause of ending the lynch mobs. The practice would have been even bloodier if not for the heroic and consistent work of mostly Black activists, social justice organizations, scholars, journalists, historians, educators, writers, clergy, and descendants of the murdered victims.

In our current era, our culture has moved forward to begin the process of truth, healing, and reconciliation regarding the violence and terror that occurred during slavery and following the Civil War. Two such places dedicated to racial reconciliation are the Monument for Peace and Justice and the Legacy Museum. Both are part of the work of the Equal Justice Initiative (EJI) in Montgomery, Alabama. When you visit EJI's national memorial, it exposes you to our nation's history of White supremacy and the acts of racial terrorism it inspired. Telling the truth in the historical narrative of human events in the past and present is the only way to heal from the repercussions of this terror.

Empathy

Amending the historical narrative to include previously omitted facts allows individuals in the community to experience empathy for events and people they may have not even known. We come together in our empathy for one another. We find that empathy by listening to each other's stories.

Every month brings another story in our communities of the harm we continue to let happen because of unequal and discriminatory practices that flow from and reinforce structural racism. Those who believe this period of systemic racism in our shared history has passed need only do a deep read about the fourteen days of abandonment of the White poor and Black Americans during and after Hurricane Katrina in 2014 in New Orleans. Or read the statistics on who died in the first six months of the COVID pandemic. The patterns and links are undeniable.

"Raise Up," by Hank Willis Thomas, stands on the rear side of the grounds of the National Memorial for Peace and Justice. Based on a photo of South African miners being subjected to a humiliating medical exam, it evokes American scenes of police suspects lined up at gunpoint.

The intergenerational trauma felt by Black Americans today is, in part, a natural human response to centuries of abandonment, of communities and social institutions treating an entire class of people as not human. Black Americans are often invisible to those with resources and ways to minimize or eliminate suffering. I have awareness and empathy for that hard, cruel fact because I have empathy for others and for myself. And I have empathy because my recovery after my own trauma was made possible by people who gave direct empathy and aid to me. I know what I felt during the times of vulnerability, recovery, and resilience in my

own lived experience, and I can identify those experiences and talk about them when needed, in the proper context, and with trusted others who may be fellow survivors of trauma.

I know firsthand the immense value of sharing your own story of loss and how you received aid, support, and understanding in times of need. Trauma and abandonment for any victim of harsh circumstances feel similar, if not the same. If we try to silence crucial, intimate facts about our most cherished wounds and truth, sickness and more harm follows as sure as night follows day. Perhaps most importantly, my empathy for myself and others leads me to identify with those who are about to be unjustly executed rather than with a so-called just executioner. All humans experience suffering and vulnerability in their life journeys; only the most dangerous among us deny this and try to claim otherwise.

A desire for empathy is the driver and the outcome of putting ourselves into another's life experience. This involves solidarity, respect, and listening to the descendants of lynching victims and those who knew them. Justice is forever denied to those who were lynched. But expressing empathy and learning the story, while commemorating the victim, can be the beginning of equality and accountability in other more modern legal situations as well. There are connections between this history of racial injustice and the lingering systemic injustice we face today. As Shirah Dedman, a descendant of a lynching victim, put it, "The point of these lynchings, at the time, was that there was no accountability. To have accountability—that would completely change the Black experience in America. And it could change the fact that as a Black American, you don't expect justice."

Reconciliation

As a part of the commitment to a complete and accurate narrative of Black American history, the racial justice movement in our society today advocates the value of diverse voices. Since they first arrived in America, people of color have recorded and shared their truth about their past and their lived experiences. In listening empathetically to these witnesses, our American narrative becomes more honest, inclusive, and fair.

The photographs and stories of the four lynchings included in this book reveal how the legacy of racial violence and terror lives on in this country today. Interviews with the victims, descendants, and their cultural descendants

When you visit EJI's national memorial, it exposes you to our nations's history of White supremacy and the acts of racial terrorism it inspired. It includes hundreds of jars of soil and steel monuments that dangle in the air.

Inside the Legacy Museum, located across from the National Memorial for Peace and Justice, hundreds of jars are displayed. They contain the soil from documented lynching sites across the country. Each is marked with the victim's name and date of death.

PHOTO: EZE AMOS, C-VILLE WEEKLY

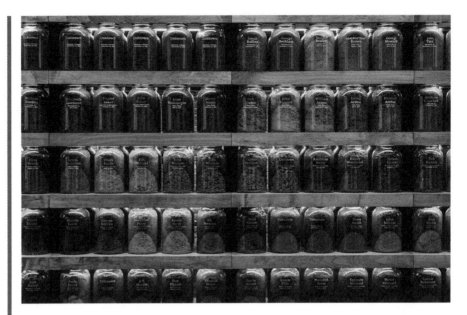

must be included in our shared American story. Amending the narrative this way is a form of racial reconciliation and can also be a way to repair the past.

The four communities in this book have all conducted a community remembrance ceremony for the lynching victim killed in their community. Community members in the local area have done research to find the present-day location where the lynching took place. In some cases, a diverse, multi-racial, multi-generational group of community members located descendants or cultural descendants to be involved with the remembrance.

Two

Acknowledgment

The Story of Charlotte Harris (1878)

In 1878, Charlotte Harris was a domestic servant who worked for a farmer, Henry Sipes, and his family in McGaheysville, Virginia, in the Shenandoah Valley. The family also held a fourteen-year-old boy named Jim Argenbright, a farmhand who also worked for the Sipes'. In the years preceding and during the Civil War, Harrisonburg and surrounding Rockingham County in western Virginia had fewer enslaved Black people than the Piedmont and eastern areas of Virginia for several reasons. During these years, approximately 700 enslaved people lived in the Shenandoah Valley compared to approximately 2,300 in neighboring Albemarle County, where farms and plantations needed slave labor to work the crops and labor in the fields. The topography and weather in western Virginia made tobacco farming untenable, but there were several plantations and farms in Rockingham County and surrounding areas where enslaved individuals were held, bred, traded, and sold. One such plantation, the Charles Yancey Plantation, still stands just two miles from where Harris worked for the Sipeses. This farm was the home of Jourden Banks, an escaped formerly enslaved person who wrote a lengthy and rich narrative of his experiences and the history of the Rockingham area, which survived and was published. This account formed the basis of the recent play, Not Made for This, which was performed at the site of the plantation. Descendants of the Banks' enslaved family and cultural descendants of the White plantation

> "The world cannot be **healed** in the abstract... Healing begins where the wound was made."
>
> —Alice Walker, *The Way Forward Is with a Broken Heart*

owner Charles Yancey researched and worked together on the production. Some of those details aided in the research of the Harris lynching and context of the times.

In 1878, Harris worked in McGaheysville, Virginia, as a domestic servant. The newspapers from the time report that she was accused of instigating a young boy, Jim Argenbright, to burn her former employer's barn. Upon learning of the fire and the accusation, the papers state she fled for four days across the Blue Ridge Mountains to take shelter with a family friend, Henry Banks. Banks lived in western Albemarle County in the Earlysville community. When the Sipes family learned from the young boy that Harris had "put him up to it," she was hunted down by a search party of three men and captured at the home of Banks. This is the narrative woven through all the papers of the day.

That was thirteen years after emancipation and the Thirteenth Amendment had freed the enslaved Black people. Slave narratives from the time tell of the same variation in treatment of enslaved Black people, as was common in all the southern states. Some reports before and after her lynching suggest that Harris was unhappy working for the Sipes family and sought to leave.

The fire occurred on the evening of February 28, 1878. The accounts in the papers describe more about the losses and monetary damage sustained in the fire than they do about Harris, the victim of the lynch mob. To this day, her descendants have not been identified. We know from courthouse records that three men were paid to apprehend her and bring her back to Harrisonburg to stand trial. On the evening of Tuesday, March 5, they allegedly arrived at the Banks' home across the mountain in Earlysville. They found her and returned with her to McGaheysville. The three men arrived with their prisoner in Rockingham County and placed her in an outbuilding on the property of her former employer, Sipes, in McGaheysville, Virginia, thirteen miles from Harrisonburg. The newspaper account states she was jailed after a hearing of sorts where 100 White citizens showed up to watch and scream their protests and instigations to punish without trial or sentence. No record of this hearing survived, and the court records are blank for the seven days surrounding these activities. On the night of March 5, the crowd dispersed, and Harris was held to await a hearing for the alleged crime, supposedly to be held the following day.

At approximately 11 p.m., two men appeared at the front of the building with cocked revolvers, demanding the guards release Harris from her jail cell. According to the accounts published in the local paper, the two armed men

The Charlotte Harris Historical Marker found at the National Memorial in Montgomery, Alabama. A community remembrance project is a sacred process, culminating in a more accurate historical account and shared experience.

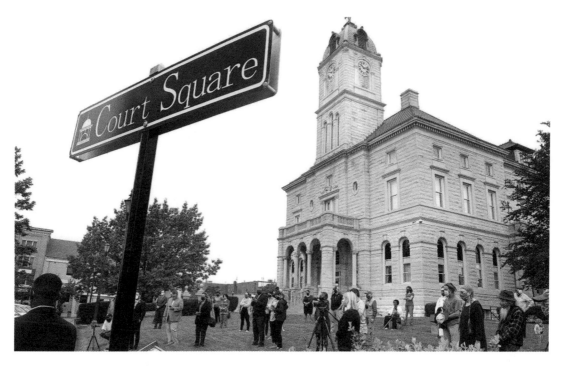

"informed the guard that if they surrendered her peaceably, it would be well for them; if not, they must take the consequences." The events are consistent with mob rule and unquestioned vigilante justice, which was common in 100 documented lynchings throughout Virginia during these years.[2]

This distraction technique, followed by a mob rush, is a tactic used for lynchings of the time. The moment that the original two armed men demanded her release, at least nine other armed men stormed the building. They were all dressed in black with black masks to disguise their appearances and to deliberately appear to be Black men. After seizing the building, they grabbed Harris and drug her out of the room. The disguised party took her about 400 yards from the jail and hung her in a tree.

The papers reported the events as follows:

They used a peculiar sort of tree, known as a Black Jack, because of its toughness. It was bent low and the rope was attached to the tree. The tree was held in its bent position until the other end of the rope was fastened to the woman's neck. In another instant, the tree was let go and the victim was jerked into midair, where in a few moments she expired, and the disguised lynchers dispersed. It was an awful penalty for the crime of which she had been accused, the like of which has hardly ever been heard of in a civilized community.[3]

From historical accounts, opinions on the Harris lynching were different in the North. An editorial printed in the New York papers on April 17, 1878, bears the headline, "An Innocent Woman Cruelly Hanged By Masked Men." In it, the writer states the following:

The details of the atrocious deed are horrible. The poor woman was pursued, captured, brought before a magistrate, and committed for trial. That night, a party of ruffians with blackened faces rushed the room and, after dragging her about a mile, hung her in a most horrible manner. Her body remained suspended from the tree from the sixth of March until noon on the ninth, when it was finally cut down. The governor issued a proclamation for the arrest of the murderers, but owing to the existing secrecy maintained by the lynchers and the public sympathy for them, none of them have been arrested.[4]

On March 16, 1878, the governor of Virginia offered a $100 reward for the capture of Harris's lynchers. About ten days later, several papers printed that a grand jury in Rockingham County was unable to identify any parties responsible for the lynching. Argenbright, the young boy accused of burning the Sipes barn, was acquitted of all charges on April 16, 1878. Newspaper accounts from Rockingham County, Alexandria, Staunton, and other cities tell the story of Harris's lynching as a national event of shame and horror.

Her body remained hanging by the side of the road for three days until it was cut down and interred. Four weeks later, a hearing acquitted the young boy of all charges. The Sipes family, who owned the barn, admitted it was the boy who set fire to it, but he escaped punishment of any sort. Researchers at the Racial Terror: Lynching in Virginia research project found fourteen newspaper stories from the year 1878 containing reports of the arrest of Harris on charges that she burned Sipes's barn. But newspaper accounts

On September 26, 2020, in Harrisonburg, Virginia, after three years of planning, research, and community work by local officials and Black activists, Charlotte Harris was commemorated. A prominent state-sponsored historical marker stands in front of the courthouse in the county where officials failed to deliver justice according to the laws of her time. Dozens of citizens came to pay respects and say her name.

PHOTO: MIKE TRIPP, THE HARRISONBURG CITIZEN

of lynchings during these times may only suggest facts and evidence. More likely, newspaper reports on lynching events from the late 1800s are problematic at best.

Supposedly, Harris had a hearing on charges that she burned Sipes's barn. But details of this arrest and hearing were never specified or recorded with the court in the official court minute book. When researching the minute book for Rockingham County, Virginia, for February through May 1878, we found that the record goes blank for the ten-day period from February 28 to March 9. Later in the record, the clerk writes that three men were reimbursed for expenses for travel and for arresting the prisoner, "CH." They were reimbursed for two days of travel, a wagon, and a horse. It is recorded that she was jailed in an outbuilding on Sipes's property. The pages contain no notes for the ten days surrounding the day she was lynched by an angry mob.

Research continues to this day on who Harris actually was. Did she have any children? Was she married? Was she previously enslaved or had she been freed? Where did the search party go to retrieve her? If it was Earlysville, as the papers state, why isn't this written in the court's minute book? And why did the authorities, and the Sipes family, seem to want Argenbright to blame her for setting the fire? The boy had a trial, and his trial is recorded in the minute book. Judge Charles O'Ferrall, the presiding judge for all matters in Rockingham County at the time, is recorded on May 14 as stating he did not believe Harris would have been convicted if she had gone to trial. Why did he make that statement for the record?

When there is no legitimate judicial investigation, the entire public is denied the actual story. We are denied proper security, protection, and equal justice according to the law. The year was 1878. Harris should have had a legal right to a hearing and a trial, but she was not afforded one. It should be in the Rockingham County record book, but it is not. Instead, she was murdered by a mob, and the record was hidden or never existed at all.

Researchers and genealogists are still searching for the real Harris. This story is not finished. Further investigation could uncover her descendants. In honor of her memory, we continue to pursue the truth.

To date, some members of the community remain angry about Harris's supposed grudge against the Sipes family. There are those who are convinced that she put Argenbright up to setting the fire. Lost in the story is the fact that Harris was not guilty of burning the barn.

Charlotte Harris' body remained hanging by the side of this country road for three days until it was cut down and interred. Researchers have located her burial site and continue to search for her descendants.

Collective Healing

Some members of local towns have done research to find the present-day location where Harris's lynching took place. In Harrisonburg, after three years
of planning, research, and community work by local officials and Black activists, Harris was commemorated. A prominent state-sponsored historical
marker stands in front of the courthouse in the county where officials failed
to deliver justice according to the laws of the time. On September 26, 2020,
the Northeast Neighborhood Association of Harrisonburg, working with
the Virginia Department of Historical Resources, the City of Harrisonburg,

Rockingham County Board of Supervisors, and the Equal Justice Initiative, conducted a ceremony on Court Square in downtown Harrisonburg to commemorate the event of her extrajudicial racial terror lynching. Local representatives of the county board of supervisors and the city council were present, and dozens of citizens came to pay respects and say her name.

We must remember the victims of lynching because when they were alive, others did not see them and did not remember them. In some of these cases, where a committee, group, or coalition has conducted remembrance ceremonies, a diverse, multi-racial, multi-generational group of community members located descendants or cultural descendants to be involved with the remembrance. These concerned citizens have participated in a community remembrance of the lynching victim and continue to do so every year. Community remembrance of the victims of racial terror lynchings may bring a deeper, more permanent change in our memory, beliefs, and feelings about our history of racial injustice and racialized trauma.

One definition of race-based trauma is witnessing ethno-violence or discrimination against another person. This witness experience may involve viewing or learning of a historical event, or it may be a personal memory of racism, institutional racism, micro-aggressions, or the constant threat of racial discrimination. Although we must set the record straight and tell the truth about racial violence, there is an emotional impact in retelling the story that can be devastating, enraging, and traumatic. Community remembrance projects are a sacred process, culminating in a more accurate account and shared experience. The story may trigger more wounds; it is only healed in voluntary community with others.

Beloved Community

What is the concept of Beloved Community? Since American philosopher and scholar Josiah Royce wrote of this idea in 1890, John Lewis, Dr. Martin Luther King Jr., and others have believed in a community where there is a real-life "kingdom" controlled by the law of love. In this model, the concept of the Kingdom of God is understood theologically but realized practically in the real world through specific actions. Dr. King speaks of the Beloved Community in the following speech.

> The dream is one of equality of opportunity. Of privilege and property widely distributed; a dream of a land where men will not take necessities from the many to give luxuries to the few; a dream of a land where men do not argue that the color of a man's skin determines the content of his character; a dream of a place where all our gifts and resources are held not for ourselves alone but as instruments of service for the rest of humanity; the dream of a country where every man will respect the dignity and worth of all human personality; and men will dare to live together as brothers.[5]

For more than fifty years, racial justice advocates have been incorporating this idea into their mission. Members of prayer circles and other groups dedicated to justice have been using radical love and acceptance to drown hatred and violence in the waters of shared humanity.

Coming to the Table

In her essay, "The Way Forward is With a Broken Heart," writer Alice Walker observes this: "The world cannot be healed in the abstract. Healing begins where the wound was made."[6] Coming to the Table (CTTT) is a group with a mission similar to the mission of the Community Remembrance Project. CTTT describes their mission as "taking America beyond the legacy of enslavement." The idea for this organization originated in 2006 at the first-ever family reunion of Sally Hemings's descendants held at Monticello. Sally Hemings was enslaved at Monticello and the mother of six of Thomas Jefferson's children. Until the arrival of DNA verification in the 1990s, the Hemings cousins had been prevented from participating in the events, traditions, and

Held annually during Black History Month, a wreath-laying ceremony is conducted in Rockingham County at the site of the unmarked graves of fifty former slaves. The cemetery in Elkton, Virginia, and local NAACP members placed headstones marked Unknown to designate all of these graves. Community members gather for the laying of a wreath to celebrate, remember and honor those who lived and died unrecognized in life.

legacy of the founding father's estate, despite being his biological descendants. At this gathering in 2006, Susan Hutchinson, a White descendant of Jefferson, met Will Hairston, the descendant of another slaveholding family in Virginia. Hutchinson's acquaintance with him, and her meetings with her Hemings cousins, led to the founding of CTTT, a group dedicated to Dr. King's dream of "the sons of former slaves and the sons of former slaveowners" coming together to the table of brotherhood.

The mission of CTTT is of a just and truthful society that acknowledges and seeks to heal from the racial wounds of the past. The goals are informed by the theories and practices of trauma awareness and resilience, with a focus on transforming the generational transmission of historical harms into racial justice and equity. The approach is rooted in four interrelated practices:
1. Uncovering history through researching and sharing a personal, community, and national history of race;
2. Making connections across racial lines through experiential activities and events;
3. Working toward healing using dialogue, reunion, ritual, meditation, ceremony, the arts, and apology;
4. Taking action to dismantle systems of racial inequality, injustice, and oppression.
The members of this group believe that whether it's the mass incarceration of people of color or the shooting of unarmed Black and brown people by police, present-day racism is an outgrowth of the unhealed legacy of slavery.

In books like *Gather at the Table* and *Slavery's Descendants*, real-life stories are presented of what CTTT members can accomplish for those who choose to become involved. Members gather for meals, events, conferences, and other activities and share what they are learning about their ancestry and how their healing has progressed. The work is not easy. As co-founder Hairston says in the book, "Change is possible. But it takes a real act of will."

Through this type of personal encounter, engagement, and shared understanding, all folks may learn what Black folks have known for hundreds of years: In America, we all share our ancestry. We are all slavery's descendants. The people in CTTT are committed to encountering, engaging, and understanding each other, one cousin at a time.

Remembrance

The Story of Allie Thompson (1918)

Charles Allie Thompson was born on February 18, 1900, in Culpeper, Virginia. His father was Wade Thompson, born in Rappahannock County, and his mother was Ida Marshall Thompson of Culpeper County, Virginia. Just eighteen years old when he was arrested for allegedly assaulting and raping a neighboring White woman, he was lynched by a mob after three men tricked the jailers in Culpeper and removed Allie Thompson from his cell.

Prior to his arrest, he had worked as a laborer on a farm. His parents owned their farm and had lived in Northern Culpeper County since their marriage in 1890. Thompson was the middle of five children. He had an older brother, Robert Levi, an older sister, Lillian, and two younger sisters. His large family was very involved in the Culpeper community and highly regarded by many. Robert served in World War I, and Allie had registered for the draft in September, the year of his murder.

Thompson and his alleged victim, Leila Sisk, had been involved in a consensual relationship according to accounts of relatives and other impartial witnesses. Sisk was twenty-six years old, having been married at fourteen to Charlie Sisk and divorced four years later. Charlie Sisk was thirty-three years old at the time of their marriage. He had been in jail following two convictions for murder in two separate cases, but he was not mentioned in any of the reports of Thomp-

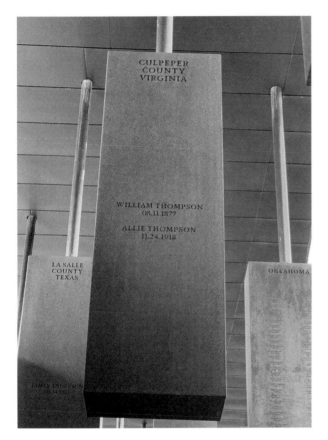

son's murder. Newspapers from the time list Sisk as married to a soldier who was overseas in France when the alleged rape occurred. Sisk and Thompson lived only one mile apart on neighboring farms. Thompson had been observed visiting Sisk in the early morning hours prior to his arrest. At around 10 a.m. on Wednesday, November 20, 1918, Deputy Sheriff E. O. Crane arrested Thompson while he was shucking corn at the farm of another neighbor. He was taken to the Culpeper jail and charged.

Several interviews with his relatives and descendants reveal key points in this tragic story: By the time Sisk met Thompson, she was no longer married. They had been seeing each other for some time. If a White woman had been known to be involved with a Black man in 1918, the lynch mob might have hanged her, too. The perpetrators of the mob murder will never be known, but given the context of the time, and the practice of hanging Black men for any actions which stepped outside the bounds of social norms in southern states, no legal protections existed for Thompson.

Later on the night of his arrest, two men went to the jail carrying a man bound in ropes. The jailers believed the men who stated that they had a prisoner wrapped in blankets who needed to be jailed. The story was a ruse to trick the jailers. The jailers asked them to take the man around to the side door. When they went to let in the men with the bundled prisoner, approximately fifteen masked men stormed the jail door, overpowered the jailers, took their keys, and removed Thompson from his cell. Reports from the papers state, "There was no disturbance, but at sunrise the body of Thompson was found dangling to a tree on the Rixleyville Road, three miles from Culpeper."[7]

Although the coroner summoned a jury to the lifeless body and held an inquest, there was no evidence as to the identity of the men in the lynching party. The case was closed with no record.

A year after Thompson was lynched, the Culpeper County Board of Supervisors voted to pay Wade Thompson, Allie's father, twenty-five dollars for a coffin and burial expenses. The family "moved on," despite the traumatic killing. Government officials declared Thompson's lynching an illegal execution. In the October 1, 1919, minutes of the meeting, the Culpeper County Board stated to his father that Thompson had been "illegally executed at the hands of unknown persons."[8]

Cultural Descendants

In 2018, descendants of Thompson and other members of his community gathered 100 years after his murder. Historian Zann Nelson describes some of these activities this way:

> The goal is to validate the families who endured this type of atrocity and were then told to just move on. We are making a commitment as a community that we want to do things differently in the future. How do we do that? By getting to know people. We pause in remembrance of these citizens who lost their lives without due process provided under the Constitution.

Filmmakers Hannah Ayers and Lance Warren have produced a short documentary, *An Outrage*, which seeks to shine a light on racial terrorism and facilitate education around it. It has been screened throughout the South, and some schools have adopted it, along with other educational materials and remembrance activities, in history and civics classes that cover racial justice and Black history. "For us, it was important to make this history personal, to talk to descendants of lynching victims and to activists about what lynching means and why we need to learn about it,"[9] Ayers said.

Community Education

Community education focused on reconciliation can improve understanding of a shared history. As our memories are expanded to include a more comprehensive, factual, and honest Black history, a community can choose change

The Allie Thompson historical marker hanging at the National Memorial in Montgomery, Alabama.

In 2018, one hundred years after Allie Thompson's lynching, Culpeper community members gathered for a memorial ceremony to learn about it, to apologize to his descendants and to work together to amend history and break the silence around racial violence and extrajudicial killings.

PHOTO: ALLISON BROPHY CHAMPION, CULPEPER STAR EXPONENT

and healing. We can achieve a new past and an expanded sense of equal justice and collective mercy. These experiences may be an invitation to heal the wounds of racial division and systemic injustice that persist today.

Healing

The Story of John Henry James (1898)

It is 2018, and two women are crouching over a plot of land near a railroad track, collecting soil from sacred ground. As they turn the soil, the brutal details fade away. No more headlines of "Colored Brute Lynched" or "Negro Fiend Hung." They use a trowel to pour soil into gallon-size glass jars with a man's name and a date etched on the front. For more than a year, in a shared pursuit with other caring and interested citizens, they have been immersed in the story of John Henry James.

James was a Black man who was lynched in Charlottesville on July 12, 1898, and then forgotten. The communities of Charlottesville, Virginia, and Albemarle County are learning of James's lynching as they develop a more full and inclusive Charlottesville history and take part in the remembrance of this forgotten man.

During the remembrance ceremony at the site of James's death, mourners read poems and offered prayers. The Black mourners present were invited to state the names of ancestors and friends they wished had seen this day. The names kept coming, and a healing circle was established by telling the stories of all the victims of justice denied—victims these witnesses had carried in their hearts.

Newspaper accounts from the time all allege the same set of claims. As stated in the Iowa County Democrat, "The negro John Henry James criminally assaulted Miss Julia Hotopp on the public road near her home on Monday morning."[10]

"Here is what I would like for you to know: In America, it is **traditional** to destroy the black body—it is heritage."

—Ta-Nehisi Coates

Very little is known about James before he was lynched. He lived in Charlottesville for approximately five years after moving to town by himself, possibly from Pennsylvania. Some community members referred to him as "the negro we knew who used to sell Hokey Pokey ice cream in the park."[11] On July 11, 1898, this local ice cream vendor was apprehended and accused of felonious assault of a young woman.

Hotopp was a twenty-year-old White woman from one of the county's most prominent families. She told her family and the authorities she was assaulted and raped near the front gate of her estate in Pen Park after returning home from running errands in town. Her father, William Hotopp, was the founder and owner of the Monticello Wine Company, the largest winemaking company in the county. Julia Hotopp reported being approached by "a very black man who was heavy set, with a slight mustache and who was wearing dark clothes and shoes with toes cut out." The news of the incident quickly spread, and around noon, James was immediately arrested with no cause or evidence but because he "somewhat fit the description" of Hotopp's assailant.[12] He was arrested at Dudley's Barroom on East Main Street near Vinegar Hill and taken to the Hotopp estate so the victim could identify her attacker.

Hotopp's brother, Carl, reportedly found his sister after her encounter with the unknown Black man. She had told him she resisted to the extent of scratching his neck. Her resistance was so effective that the would-be assailant failed to "accomplish his foul purpose."[13]

After Hotopp identified James, he was jailed in Charlottesville. A mob of enraged White people had already gathered outside the jail and were shouting open threats, demanding a lynching. So, shortly after his arrest, police officers slipped the prisoner out the back door of the jail and sent him to Staunton, forty miles west, for safekeeping. The next morning, James was charged with rape and criminal assault after a special grand jury convened in Charlottesville. The prisoner was summoned to return to Charlottesville the next day to face charges. The judge, commonwealth's attorney, and sheriff attempted to guard the man and return him safely to receive a fair trial, but "the lynching party outgenerated the authorities," according to the Newport News Daily.[14]

The following day, James was aboard a train bound for Charlottesville when the train slowed to avoid a decoy on the tracks. The decoy was a man, dressed as a woman, flagging down the train in mock distress. One eyewitness to the raid from Waynesboro gave this account: "There were 100 men on horse-

Siri Russell and Jalane Schmidt collect soil from the site where John Henry James was lynched.

PHOTO: MICHAEL WILLIAMSON, WASHINGTON POST

23

back with their pistols drawn. The leader commanded the men guarding the prisoner, 'Gentlemen, we want this Negro.'"

The angry mob then boarded the train. They placed three ropes around James's neck and dragged him to a nearby tree at Woods Crossing near Charlottesville. Reportedly, as news spread about the attack, a group of Black men assembled with plans to stop the lynching, but they were outnumbered by the White mob, and James was hanged. Members of the mob then fired seventy rounds of bullets into his dead body. Carl Hotopp was at the scene and was observed shooting the body after it was hung. Because James was hung in sight of the passenger train and other trains passing on the tracks, the event became a public spectacle lynching. His killing was celebrated by several hundred more White people who gathered to see his body as it was left hanging for hours. They collected souvenirs from the scene, including pieces of the tree and of James's clothing.

In the weeks following the lynching, many newspapers made James out to be a "beast deserving of death" for having defiled an innocent White woman. His indictment claimed, without proof, that he "did ravish and carnally know against her will and by force" the White woman, Hotopp.[15] But Hotopp and her brother Carl both told the authorities that she successfully resisted James's attempts to assault her.

Was it an assault, a greeting, an attempt to approach, or a glance? Because no due process of a trial or hearing ever happened, we cannot know the answer for certain. What is known is that John Henry James was hanged because of an accusation of assault. He died proclaiming his innocence. His supposed victim stated she successfully resisted his alleged assault, as did her brother. The man's life and story were overshadowed in the papers by the city's struggle to decide whether lynching should be against the law.

At the time of the murder, local papers wrote this: "We believe the authorities were blamable. They knew it was risky to bring this man unprotected to Charlottesville. His troubles are over. Those of the community have just begun." Over 100 years later, it is also clear that most of the citizens of Charlottesville and Albemarle County approved of the lynch mob's actions. One paper wrote that the lynching may have been best because it spared Hotopp the "terrible ordeal of a public trial."[16]

The lynch mob who killed James did not conceal their identity. Late in the day of the lynching, after his body had hung for hours in view of all peo-

Community members gather and pray during the ceremony to collect soil from the site of John Henry James's lynching.

PHOTO: EZE AMOS, CHARLOTTESVILLE TOMORROW

ple who would receive the message of terror, the sheriff ordered it to be cut down and his body interred by the authorities. On the morning of July 13, a coroner's jury convened, and the members found that James died either from hanging or gunshot wounds and that he "came to his death by the hands of persons unknown to the jury."[17]

If James had family back in Pennsylvania who sought then, or now, to discover what happened to him, they were not likely to get much help from the authorities in their quest for the truth. The authorities participated in denying the known lynchers who had murdered with impunity. But the lynchers boldly left their identities uncovered, and the authorities were present at the scene of this lynching.

During the era of racial terror lynchings, it was quite common for groups of White citizens to impulsively claim charges of sexual assault against Black men, even when such accusations were unsubstantiated, denied, or retracted by the women involved. This practice regularly triggered violent White mobs, and the cycle of hysteria and delusion culminated in the lynchings of innocent Black men.

The authorities in Charlottesville and Albemarle sought to strengthen White supremacy and justify the White mob that took the law into their

own hands. In describing James, a man they did not know or seek to know, as a tramp, a black brute, and perhaps a valued member of the chain gang, the officials thought they could control alleged criminal offenders and cast Black men as perpetual criminal assailants. Lynchings that involved large, unmasked mobs were intended to convey a message of fear and terror to the Black community.

Ceremonies and Monuments

James's life, and his death by hanging, was forgotten until 2015. That year, James's story was included with about 4,400 other lynchings at the National Memorial for Peace and Justice in Montgomery, Alabama. In 2018, after a collaborative process of research, study, and activism, citizens of Charlottesville gathered soil from an area known as Woods Crossing near the site of the lynching. The glass jar containing the sacred soil from this location was taken, pilgrimage-style, to the memorial in Montgomery, Alabama.

The Jefferson School African American Heritage Center in the Vinegar Hill community of Charlottesville led the group of local citizens as they carried the soil collected from the site of James' death. The group will soon install a coffin-size memorial at the Albemarle County Courthouse near Justice Park in Charlottesville. The National Monument for Peace and Justice, a part of the mission of the Equal Justice Initiative, holds these coffin-size stone markers for the 400 counties in the United States where a documented lynching or lynchings took place. Upon completion of the marker and memorialization and commemoration activities, local community members bring one marker back while the other hangs on the grounds of EJI's massive monument to the slain victims of the era of racial terror. The community remembrance projects are a way to make visible a past that has previously been denied. It is an effort to honor a man and a people who were seeking to live together peacefully and equally under the protection and care of the law.

Black Settlements

How do we move away from a community of dominance and grow into a community of care? This evolution may be hastened by increasing the historical preservation of Black places and stories. The Legacy Museum in Montgomery, Alabama, and the National Monument for Peace and Justice are two such places. But these are not the only public memorials dedicated to telling the full story of racial violence in the United States. There are several such enlightening and educational places in every region of our country.

In Philadelphia, at the Lest We Forget Museum in Germantown, the curators have collected an immense exhibition of artifacts and interpretive exhibits that teach about the lives of enslaved people and their centuries-long struggle to be free.

In Washington, D.C., the National Museum of African American History and Culture is our nation's comprehensive collection of documents and exhibits showcasing the African American story and its impact on American and world history.

Dr. Brenda Brown-Grooms listens deeply to the remarks at the memorial and is moved to tears.

PHOTO: MICHAEL WILLIAMSON, WASHINGTON POST

In Detroit, Michigan, the Charles H. Wright Museum educates and enlightens citizens on the true history of Black enslavement and the struggle for freedom.

The Whitney Plantation in Louisiana has accepted the challenge of reworking public tours that offer the complete story about a plantation in antebellum Louisiana and the experience of the enslaved during and after the Civil War. The staff and directors of the Whitney Plantation have created art where terror used to reign; their staff and advisers are led by educators and activists who present the lived experience of slaves and slave owners to create a shared and accurate record of the history of the place.

And in McGaheysville, Virginia, the Charles Yancey Plantation sits only five miles from the site of the lynching of Charlotte Harris. The plantation's name is RiverBank, and the current owners are thoughtful, proactive, and serious about their responsibility to engage in community awareness and education about what life was truly like at this place, the site of a home that once owned more than fifty slaves. Each year, the Shenandoah Valley Black Heritage Project (SVBHP) produces festivals, dramatic presentations, and cultural events to celebrate Black heritage. In 2018, at the RiverBank Charles Yancey site, SVBHP presented the play Not Made for This, based on the narrative of escaped former slave Jourden Banks. The play was written by Brianna Olivares Madden, a young intern at the SVBHP office.

Historians believe slavery, the Civil War, Reconstruction, and lynching are interrelated parts of the same historical narrative. One premise of this book is that there are modern-day remnants of White supremacy and violence toward democratic norms that trace a legacy back to Reconstruction. As a result, Black communities have suffered disenfranchisement, mob violence, abandonment, racial massacres, and loss. Reconstruction was followed by the politicized reversal of gains made in protection of Black citizens and equality. Wherever a lynching occurred in the United States, a Black settlement was present nearby. Places where Black families lived, worked, celebrated life, and tried to survive and protect each other. For James, that community was most likely Vinegar Hill. The twenty-acre plot of land known as Vinegar Hill near downtown Charlottesville lies between the university and the main business district. In the 1870s, former slaves settled there following emancipation. By the 1940s and 1950s, the neighborhood had grown into a dynamic community of Black businesses serving Black customers and others. The formerly enslaved in the 1890s hoped that land and homeownership

More than 100 years after his death, this marker hangs at the EJI monument in Montgomery, Alabama and in Charlottesville, Virginia to acknowledge James publicly.

and entrepreneurship would guarantee progress for them and their families. Hard work and progress proved them right throughout the era of racial violence, Jim Crow laws, and other challenges.

In 1898, when James was living and working as an ice cream vendor in the area, he was undoubtedly a part of a community that would eventually grow into a thriving neighborhood with thirty Black-owned businesses and 140 Black family homes. There was a fish market, tailor, barbershop, and popular jazz nightclub. Local Black residents had a clothing store, a drug store, restaurants, a school, and insurance agencies.

But in the 1950s, urban renewal projects began appearing throughout the country under the auspices of federally sponsored legislation to enable commercial development in so-called slums and blighted areas. The history shows that White community leaders deemed Black settlements and commercial and residential districts attractive for real estate and commercial ventures. Business developers in localities like Charlottesville were allowed to claim residents' property through eminent domain and other laws to make way for the destruction of Black-owned businesses and homes against the will of residents in the area. In Charlottesville, residents tried to organize to save their homes and the businesses and neighborhood of Vin-

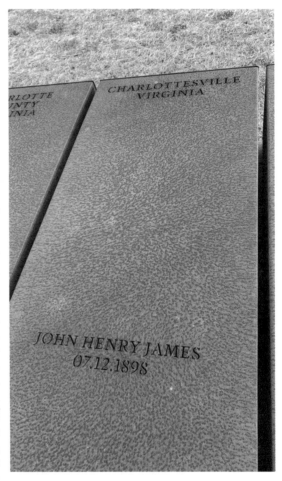

egar Hill, but when the matter came up for a local vote, a poll tax prevented Black citizens of modest means from voting their interests to defeat the urban renewal that razed the Vinegar Hill district. In 1960, the bulldozers destroyed the community. Although residents received modest living accommodations in publicly funded or subsidized housing, the bonds, cohesion, and pride of place that evolved in their beloved Vinegar Hill were gone forever.

Back in 1878, James was treated with a similar disregard of the law or any common understanding of human rights. The Fourteenth Amendment to the United States Constitution had made James a citizen. Yet, was he truly an American citizen with all the rights and equality citizenship implies? Did he and the other Black citizens of Charlottesville in that era have equal access on a personal and a systemic level to justice, opportunity, health, safety, and due process under the law? In current times, although the fire of vigilante justice no longer burns as hot, can we really claim that the embers do not linger?

While completing research and reading for this book, I returned repeatedly to moments in history when these struggles could have been resolved. Instead of a permanent achievement of basic human rights for Black people, the gains made were incremental; just as often, they were temporary. Every man, woman, and child strives to live in solidarity and safety in community with others. Since 1619, Black people settled peacefully in every county where racial terror lynchings occurred. In cases of the lynching events told in the stories in this book, victims of racial violence and terror were trying to escape domination, violence, and oppression and live peacefully as productive, loving members of their communities.

From the time the first slave ships arrived in America, Africans have been enslaved but never mastered. From the start, the resilience and resistance of Black Americans has been relentless. To discover the forgotten places where they made a home and a way of life for their families is to encounter this timeless truth. None of us will ever stop fighting for the equality and freedom of our own people. If we receive these stories with an open mind and a genuine, caring curiosity and empathy, we may discover our common value systems and shared history. The value system referred to here is a mutual respect for basic human rights and equal treatment under the law. This is a universal human value system that includes reverence for the sanctity of human life and a commitment to honesty and accountability for harms done. It contains the principle of equal access to opportunities in all social spheres of living. It enshrines a common value of freedom from abuse and discrimination and equal access to legal redress in the case of proven discrimination. With knowledge and a commitment to this shared value system, we may more easily agree on whom to memorialize. We may come to learn how to teach a shared history without judgment: a history based on these common human rights and values.

A community member adds soil from the community collection ceremony to the memorial in Alabama.

PHOTO: JULIE BENNETT/ USA TODAY NETWORK

Change

The Story of Frazier Baker (1898)

Within days of his murder in a horrendous fire set by an angry mob at his home, Frazier Baker's lynching garnered national attention. His appointment to the position of postmaster in Lake City, South Carolina, was made because President William McKinley sought political favor in the southern states. The president, and his political allies in South Carolina, believed the job needed to go to a qualified Black citizen. In fact, McKinley had appointed hundreds of Black individuals to postmasterships across the southern United States during his remaining tenure as a part of patronage jobs to build local networks.

Baker was an educated, hardworking man—a forty-two-year-old schoolteacher. He had experience serving his community as a postmaster in a neighboring Black town, and he was willing to continue to serve. Like many other African American lynching victims, Baker was not accused of or guilty of rape, theft, assault, or any other crime. He had become a target of violence and terror solely based on his race and for serving in a prominent position reserved in past decades for Whites only.

The majority White population of Lake City, South Carolina, could not allow a Black man to hold a position of authority. So, when Baker attempted to accept the presidential appointment and do his job, they killed him. They also burned down his home while his family slept, setting a fire along the back wall of the Baker home. This ensured the husband, wife, and six children would awaken and try to flee out the front door.

When the family awoke in the night to a burning house, Baker stood at the front door as they shot him and his one-year-old infant daughter, Julia. The mob injured his wife and two of the other children as they sought escape through the front door. In her trial testimony and her statement to authorities after the murders, Baker's wife, Lavinia, described her husband as he opened the door to run to safety: Seeing the mob of armed men, he shouted, "We might as well die running as standing still!"[18]

Baker had been a successful postmaster for several years in the nearby all-Black town of Effingham, South Carolina. He was an educated and respected member of his community. Besides being a schoolteacher, he had been a farmer and treasurer of the Colored Farmers' Alliance in Florence County, South Carolina. He became a postmaster of the Effingham Post Office in Florence County on March 15, 1892, and held the position until November 1894.

Frazier Baker's widow, Lavinia Baker, is seen in this portrait with her five surviving children, Sarah, Lincoln, Willie, Cora, and Rosa. Through the activism and charity of supporters, she remained in Charleston during the trial for Frazier Baker's accused killers.

PHOTO: LIBRARY OF CONGRESS

But none of these qualifications mattered to the White townspeople who decided a Black man attempting to be their postmaster must be uppity and incompetent. When threats and attempted shootings did not work to intimidate Baker, an angry mob torched his home in the middle of the night just five months after he took office. The mob thought their action would put an end to the situation. The day after the fire, on February 23, 1898, the Charleston News and Courier described Lake City as "a white man's town, not over a dozen negroes living in the place, and not one would ever believe it was acceptable to attempt to serve in a position of authority."[19]

What constituted a lynching during the era of racial terror? Most people believe that lynching is defined as a hanging, but lynching means much more. Lynching is the killing of African Americans who were tortured, mutilated, burned, shot, dragged, or hanged. The victims were accused of an alleged

crime by a White mob and deprived of their lives without due process and equal protection of the law.

In the aftermath of the killings of Baker and his daughter, Julia, Black townspeople were outraged. They took action by organizing mass meetings and petitioning the federal government to bring charges against the suspected killers. A fourteen-month investigation led to indictments, and over a year later, twelve men stood trial for arson, murder, and conspiracy to kill a government employee. The trial was quite a spectacle, lasting two weeks and gaining coverage across the region from many newspapers. The older Baker children testified as well as Frazier's wife, Lavinia. Three members of the mob who burned the Baker home turned on the other men, provided evidence, and admitted their involvement.

But in the middle of the trial, the proceedings were halted as a special investigator was summoned from the attorney general's office in Washington, D.C. In the end, four of the men were found not guilty, and the jury could not convict the other five defendants. An unsatisfactory outcome for Black members of the community of Lake City; the effects were to be felt for generations to come. The federal government used the Enforcement Acts to prosecute the mob members. In 1898, a civil rights activist named Ida B. Wells was becoming known for her anti-lynching crusade. Her mission was comprehensive. Her passion was personal and unmatched, having lost three dear friends to a lynching in Memphis, Tennessee, years earlier. Because of her actions, McKinley was prompted to look into the Baker killing. The long and comprehensive investigation that led to the Baker trial ensued because the attack on the Baker home was based solely on racial prejudice and took place on federal grounds (the Baker's home was also the U.S. Post Office for Lake City, South Carolina).

At the turn of the century, in South Carolina, the context of the Baker murders before and after the lynching was replete with consequences. Because Baker held a government-appointed job, his case became the pivot point for organizers and advocates to demand change and accountability for the terrorism and crime of lynching. Yet, the driving force behind the escalation of these public massacres remained and went on unabated for fifty more years. That driving force was White mob violence. These horrific acts were directed against the entire Black community. The method was effective. In state after state in the South, economic, social, and civic progress for Black people was thwarted or reversed. In the South, in 1898, a Black man never knew if he would be the next victim. Other members of his community were terrorized into retreating from social, economic, and political gains made. Black people were conditioned, intimidated, and threatened through terrorism and violence to move back into a social compliance that resembled slavery.

Knowledge

Today, many noted and accomplished advocates, lawyers, investigators, data scientists, sociologists, journalists, and scholars are involved in the study and eradication of racial violence. One of the first of these was Wells, who was born enslaved in Mississippi in 1862, just before General Grant's troops captured her hometown of Holly Springs, Mississippi, in the Civil War. She was born just before freedom and under the watchful eye of Union soldiers. By the time she turned eighteen, the Thirteenth and Fourteenth Amendments freed her, and

On December 12, 2013, an historical marker was erected on the site of the post office where Postmaster Baker and his family were attacked in 1898.

PHOTO: DONNA TRACY, SCNOW

she was on a path to receiving her education and becoming a teacher. Wells would grow to believe in herself and her ability to get things done.

These traits were forged in hardship and loss. When she was just sixteen years old, she lost her parents to the yellow fever epidemic and assumed responsibility for raising her siblings. During her days teaching school in the 1880s, she wrote articles for local Black newspapers. She eventually quit teaching and became a full-time journalist, moving to Memphis, Tennessee.

In March 1892, three of Wells's friends were lynched in Memphis. Thomas Moss, Cal McDowell, and Will Stewart were running a successful grocery store in competition with a White-owned store across the street in a Black neighborhood in Memphis. Known as the Curve, the thriving Black community in Memphis was the site of The People's Grocery, a successful Black owned establishment. Thomas Moss owned the store and McDowell and Stewart were two of his workers. They were close friends of Wells and beloved in the community. The executions of these respected and influential Black leaders marked a breaking point that led to investigations by Wells. She wrote stories in the Memphis Free Speech which exposed the real reasons and events behind the lynchings and a week of vicious attacks on Black citizens which had preceeded the lynchings. Her advocacy was part of a larger strategy developed to use writing and journalism to respond to the trauma of the lynchings and challenge racial discrimination, inequality and violence.

Eventually, the result of this atrocious and personal loss was more activism and more writing. She wrote the pamphlet "Southern Horrors" in 1892 to catalog all lynchings; she began describing and documenting this distinctive form of large-scale, systematic racial terrorism in a scholarly way. The effort continues to this day and forms the first stage of changing the mass violence: acknowledgment and truth-telling in the story of every lynching.

Wells saw that lynching was an effort to reestablish the White supremacy that had prevailed throughout the South before the Civil War. She started her own newspaper, Free Speech, and collected data on the 728 lynchings in America over the previous ten years. By 1898, she was a prominent and well-known civil rights activist, becoming famous for her anti-lynching crusade. She was living in Chicago with her husband, prominent attorney Ferdinand Barnett, and their two children. In an action that preceded Rosa Parks, Wells protested efforts to be moved out of the White section of a railway car and came to blows with the officer attempting to remove her. The episode led to her lawsuit

The late Dr. Fostenia Baker was the great niece of Frazier Baker. She is seen here participating in the community remembrance ceremony to honor his life and heroic death.

PHOTO: DONNA TRACY, SCNOW

36

against the railway to ensure the overturning of public segregation laws. She won her case, although it was later overturned in the Supreme Court.

As a prominent member of her Chicago community, Wells investigated and reported on lynchings and other racial injustices as objectively as possible. She was involved in educating the public through fact-based, detailed journalism in the Black press. She had for ten years been organizing appeals to local, state, and federal officials on lynching practices and the violations of law such actions and practices represented.

At considerable risk to her own life and her family's well-being, Wells was well-positioned and ready to act in the days after the lynching of Baker and his daughter, Julia. Two days after the killing, a mass meeting occurred at Bethel Church in Chicago. Wells spoke about the murders and challenged government officials by name. She condemned the senators and other officeholders for remaining silent and inactive in the face of an appointed postmaster being shot down in public for the offense of holding a public office when local Whites told him not to.

McKinley was reportedly indignant about the lynching. Chicago's Republican district congressmen introduced a resolution to go before the Post Office committee to start a vigorous investigation. The United States Attorney General became directly involved in the case. Soon after, a collection was taken at Bethel for Wells to join the Illinois officials in Washington to lobby for decisive federal intervention and monetary reparations for Baker's beleaguered family. She went to Washington, and she remained involved in the charitable support of Baker's widow and children throughout her life. During the Washington, D.C., trip following the lynching, Wells addressed McKinley and expressed her desire on behalf of Black Americans that he take appropriate action to apprehend and punish Baker's lynchers and urge indemnity for the family. She also told the president that national legislation for the suppression of the federal crime of lynching was needed for nearly twenty years of lynching crimes. It was 120 years later when Ida Wells's efforts resulted in recognition of the truth of the crime, if not justice. In 2019, Representative James Clyborn and others from the Lake City, South Carolina, community hosted a community remembrance ceremony recognizing the Baker family's courage and service.

Wells's scholarship mattered. Her work mattered in the field of journalism and public education about White mob violence. And she was not the only prominent writer doing these things. In 1910, Monroe Nathan Work, one of the first professors working in the brand new scientific field of sociology, worked to catalog all known lynchings. He summarized and documented the data, which later amassed into the records that would become the Tuskegee University Database on Lynchings in America. The research collected at Tuskegee University in Tuskegee, Alabama, provides an invaluable resource, as these sources are widely viewed as the most comprehensive collection of research data about lynching in America. The Tolnay-Beck database is another comprehensive catalog of known lynchings. The extraordinary work of E. M. Beck and Stewart E. Tolnay helps today's researchers track and collect the data for all states on lynchings.

In addition to these scholarly efforts, the Equal Justice Initiative maintains a database of all known lynchings in the United States from 1877 to 1955. At James Madison University in Harrisonburg, Virginia, Dr. Gianluca De Fazio and his students collect and maintain timely data in the project known as Racial Terror: Lynching in Virginia, 1877-1927.

Advocacy

In the 1920s, the National Association for the Advancement of Colored People (NAACP) began a social campaign to affect the social conscience of the nation on the realities of lynching. They hung a banner over the street at their headquarters in New York City. They conducted public square demonstrations that were simple, stark, and moving. These efforts were designed as a means of publicly speaking out in truth and memorializing what was occurring nearly every day, especially in southern states. But the most important work of the NAACP was and still is the individual casework they conduct on behalf of any citizen who contacts them with a report of discrimination, violence, or injustice.

The effort to end lynching began to get noticed in 1892 when Ida B. Wells, a journalist, teacher, activist and social critic who had been born a slave in 1862 published "Southern Horrors: The Lynch Law in All Its Phases." She challenged the public silence that professed ignorance about ongoing lynching. Here she is pictured with her four children.

PHOTO: LIBRARY OF CONGRESS

By 1930, a legal team working within the NAACP mission and alongside community activists enacted a three-prong strategy to bring about change at the local level. This strategy was designed to dismantle segregation through three interrelated parts. First, activists worked to solidify a nationwide network of Black lawyers to file test cases against documented segregation practices. Second, these legal cases built precedential support for a direct constitutional attack against segregation through carefully targeted litigation. Third, the organization directed volunteers and workers to organize in local Black communities in unified support against ongoing discriminatory practices.

In this way, the NAACP was able to advance a court-based civil rights advocacy through a nationwide network. It also was deployed to advance an anti-lynching campaign. Wells, W. E. B. Dubois, Walter White, and many other notable Black leaders of the time educated the public and encouraged protest at the community level to lobby for federal legislation. A change in the law did result from this strategy. The Dyer Anti-Lynching Bill passed in 1922. Of course, it was later overturned. We continue to need this and more activism today. The Emmett Till Antilynching Act was finally signed into law in March of 2022, making lynching a federal hate crime.

These organizations and individuals contributed to the change that has nearly eliminated lynching in America. Experts have observed that as lynching ended, other forms of social repression of Black Americans have increased, such as mass incarceration and police killings of unarmed citizens of color. Social change, equal rights, and personal safety for all citizens do not happen without a comprehensive and accurate reporting of the problem. These outcomes follow a process of acquiring knowledge and then demonstrating an organized activism based on strategic goals. Historians now know, for instance, to check multiple sources when attempting to arrive at an accurate account of events.

Why did these stories survive if not to give us a roadmap toward a future where equality prevails? What is the reason to remember our nation's violent past? These answers matter, as there will always be critics of and barriers to remembering a painful, violent past.

But the reason to remember our shared lynching history and the victims of lynching is more than simply moral principle or a desire for justice and to do the right thing. A coexisting moral principle is seen in the desire to trans-

As a part of every community remembrance project, volunteers work together to obtain a marker which will be displayed near the lynching site and serve to educate visitors and passersby about the history of lynching.

PHOTO: DONNA TRACY, SCNOW

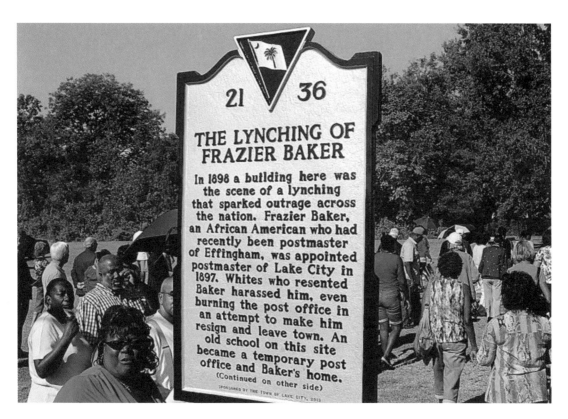

form conflict into healing and reconciliation. Cross-racial solidarity is about the future. It's about answering the question, Will we destroy each other?

The educators, journalists, and scholars writing and working together in multi-racial coalitions for the past 150 years have left some answers and methods for preserving democracy. However, it is also true that many of the necessary social changes have not even occurred. Examples of this are the needed equality in our public schools and human rights in policing. And even when inequality is addressed in the law, discrimination returns; resentment, bias, and hatred born of loss and found in the human heart will remain in individuals within our social systems. Unhealed pain, anger, resentment, and fear may lead to a righteous discriminatory identity that harms others and is not informed by facts. Scholars and students note the increase of lynchings during the brutal poverty, hunger, and joblessness that persisted for all Americans during the depression of 1930-1940. This is not to excuse systematic group violence, but solutions and understanding on all levels improves outcomes. As teacher, mother, activist, and journalist Wells often said, "Eternal vigilance is the watchword of freedom."[20]

State Commissions

The third annual state conference of the Maryland Lynching Memorial Project was held in November 2021. It was noted that in just three years, the group had grown from twenty-five attendees to a mailing list of more than 2,500 people. In commemorating the thirty-eight lynchings known to have occurred in fourteen Maryland counties, the state has erected five markers, and multiple Truth, Racial Healing & Transformation (TRHT) commissions have begun to hold community-based hearings. This is a first step toward acknowledging the stories and addressing the reparations needed for documented lynching events. Maryland, along with eleven other former slave states, is taking responsibility for the lynchings that occurred within its borders. Working in partnership with the Equal Justice Initiative, the creator of the National Memorial for Peace and Justice in Montgomery, community coalitions have erected approximately fifty EJI and state historical markers as a part of their community remembrance projects. Several of these localities then partner with state officials to form a statewide commission, as Maryland did. This has been done in Virginia, Florida, and Georgia, three of the states engaged in this type of activism. This helps researchers and teachers learn more and form links with the developing national movement to commemorate the spaces and stories of the nearly 6,500 lynching victims across the nation.

> In its training manual for TRHT projects, the W.K. Kellogg Foundation states: Memorials serve as a reminder of suffering. But memorials also remind us of the effort and strength that emerge from the suffering. When we face the truth of history, we no longer carry the pain, fear, and shame of history, for we have discovered how to look at our shared past with courage and honesty.

Pain and memory have their own spirit. To be free, to be strong, we must remember the pain, as individuals and as a society. This pain, and the experience of being vulnerable, leads to the sharing of the truth to seek justice, one story at a time.

Six

Memory

The Future Narrative

"We must truthfully **confront** our history of racial injustice before we can repair its painful legacy."

—Equal Justice Initiative

The narrative of emancipation for enslaved African Americans officially began 152 years ago from 1863-1865 with three constitutional amendments and the Emancipation Proclamation. This began, but did not ensure, the liberation of formerly enslaved Black people in the slaveholding states of the southern U.S. The narrative in 2021, when this book was written, had its origins in the civil rights movement that started in the 1950s. There was a solidifying of mission and a slowdown in community activism once the Civil Rights Act and the Voting Rights Act were signed by President Johnson in 1964 and 1965, respectively. A national experience of assassinations, extremism, and the Vietnam War also sent the violence into overdrive. You cannot study or understand the future narrative without reference points from the past and present.

Sociologists and historians have identified a third wave of the civil rights movement beginning with five pivotal events over the last twelve years. To set the context for this third wave, before these five pivotal events, two large and significant social changes occurred. First, America elected a Black president in 2008; second, due to more widespread use of mobile video and cell phone technology, the apprehension and killing of unarmed Black citizens gained public attention beyond the Black community.

This culminated in the widely publicized death of Trayvon Martin at the hands of a self-proclaimed vigilante citizen. Following a trial, the killer

was not convicted of murder despite ample evidence. Recently enacted state law to protect so-called vigilante justice provided cover. Significant and effective social justice narratives of the past and the future are written in the streets. Citizen journalists and protestors organized, and the event was followed by concerned citizens amplifying Black voices and protest through the forming of the organization, Black Lives Matter. This was the first event.

Next came the cold-blooded mass murder of five Black churchgoers in 2015 in Charleston, South Carolina. They had invited a White supremacist to pray with them during their evening Bible study. He came to their group, and then he shot and killed them. His mission was to kill Black people in a historic shrine of the civil rights movement.

A protest sign seen at an anti-racist demonstration in response to the death of George Floyd in Minneapolis in May of 2020.

PHOTO: THE BELLEVILLE NEWS DEMOCRAT

Following these murders at Mother Emanuel AME Church, social change and citizen protests led to the development of a collection of Black history known as The Charleston Syllabus. It was published and disseminated to individuals and schools as a more authentic, inclusive, and comprehensive treatment of the actual historical record of Black people's experience in the U.S. and became available to all citizens and students. This and other scholarships, such as the 1619 Project, are coalescing to offer a distinct script for the future narrative and the third wave of a U.S. civil rights movement.

The next catastrophic mass casualty event that helped solidify the modern-day narrative and point activists and citizens toward more equitable future narratives was the killing and violence in Charlottesville, Virginia, on August 12, 2017. The Charlottesville violence occurred when the organized Neo-Nazi group, Unite the Right, targeted the progressive city for an attack in the public square that injured many and killed one. Their cover was a publicized demonstration against the removal of Confederate monuments. The record shows the group planned violence and domestic terror as the main event.

Fourth, the murder of George Floyd in June 2020 at the hands of police officer Derek Chauvin spurred a summer of protests and demonstrations from civil rights activists demanding specific changes for equality and social justice. In the midst of these significant sociocultural events, pivotal event number five was the election of a candidate to the presidency who advocated violence among racial groups. He was the avowed favorite of hate groups and right-wing paramilitary groups, and he often stimulated racial prejudice and hatred with policies and hate speech that contained stereotypes and bias toward minorities.

Delusion

Leaders who encourage violence and hate are a surprise in the current narrative, but such immoral leadership is not new to American discourse. For most of us, such aggression is troubling and surprising. Yet even more puzzling is the question of who would follow such extreme movements, hate groups, and divisive leaders?

In this book, I have told the story of four people who were publicly murdered for acts they did not commit. The delusion of the inequality of humans because of their race is in the system before it is in the individual. With mass delusion of a group or collective, people experience fear (sometimes expressed in aggression or anger) and false information on a group level. If

Enslaved African men and women strain against their shackles in panicked alarm. The sculpture, by the Ghanaaian artist Kwame Akoto-Bamfo, stands at the entrance to the National Memorial for Peace and Justice in Montgomery, Alabama. The artist dedicated his work to the memory of the victims of the trans-Atlantic slave trade.

the delusion is in the system before it is in the individual, how is the delusion answered, corrected, or neutralized? An accurate fact-based accounting of events is how we answer and correct the delusion. History shows that when there is a critical mass of organized groups passionate for justice, change can happen, even amid a society where collective delusion is present.

Psychologically, in these horrific situations, we often underestimate three salient features of human behavior:

1. How good it feels to be a part of a group that shares and affirms our beliefs. The experience produces intense, joyful, passionate, and euphoric feelings. The intensity is so strong it often overrides logic and rational thought. It can be an intense driving force when we have this sense of belonging,

and it can be equally strong when we are missing it. This intense bond can include vehement hatred of other groups, which may tip into dehumanizing rhetoric and, in some cases, actions.

2. For some, the intoxicating elixir of total and complete control of events and people drives dangerous and deceitful behavior. When this happens, the stakes are everything because it allows dehumanization to occur. Control of others in this way is always abusive, destructive, threatening, and dangerous.

3. Humans who cannot feel or admit their own suffering and vulnerability can be dangerous, especially when they hold a role as a family, community, or government leader.

Without the "other" group to blame for the negative events in one's life, these individuals must attribute the cause of negative events to themselves only. When persistent and severe deprivation, poverty, and social chaos have been experienced for a long time, these individuals become desperate for a cause—any cause—that does not implicate themselves as the source or cause of their suffering.

The solution to facing the delusions of those in leadership positions is always truth. It's knowing what's true and stating it. We must protect innocent others from the harm that comes from group delusions. We must especially anticipate and intervene on situations where a delusional leader can easily harm others with control and deceit and by commanding a following and manipulating them to commit further harm.

The single most powerful tool against injustice and dangerous deceit (here called delusion) is what Bishop Michael Curry calls the Truth Force. Because there is a depth of truth and a strength of purpose in today's racial justice activism, it would seem that a new age has dawned. It comes from the streets; it is local, youth-led, and conducted in Black-led multiracial coalitions.

During the years 2015 to 2022, historians suggest we can begin to see the edge of a future narrative for racial equality emerging. Some features that may define the next stage of this movement over the coming decades include: (a) prevalent education in schools and the public culture on the concepts and vocabulary of structural racism and how to work against it; (b) awareness of decentering whiteness in U.S. social institutions and culture; (c) defining White privilege; and (d) for those members of the previously dominant European American culture, suggestions or guidelines for being an anti-racist ally to people of color.

In the early 1800s, this Alexandria, Virginia, building was owned by Charles M. Price and his partner, James Birch. They bought and sold hundreds of enslaved men, women, and children. This building allowed the firm to purchase, hold, and then ship hundreds of the enslaved at a time. Such public spaces continue to exist throughout the Southern U. S. without any public recognition of the role played in our history and in current societal struggles with structural racism.

PHOTO: LIBRARY OF CONGRESS

How do we know when the historical narrative has changed? We will know the narrative has changed toward a justice and equality narrative when all victims of racial violence are protected by law and in fact. We will know the narrative has changed toward real justice when we have, in fact and in circumstance, honored our national creed of equality for all. It is exhilarating to discover how we can come to the table to learn where we will work together.

A Purpose-Filled Life

As we learn about heroes like Ida Wells and John Lewis, we wonder, are these people different from ordinary citizens?

In one way, the answer is yes. In both cases, their courage and vision were extraordinary. But they both came from struggle, experienced intense pain, sorrow, and loss. They evolved into cultural heroes in the crucible of a community of like-minded and committed social change advocates. Any one of us can choose to evolve and grow in this way.

From 1961 to 1967, Lewis was jailed forty times during peaceful protests against the unjust suppression of voting rights and civil rights. Some of these episodes resulted in being sentenced to thirty days in the Mississippi State Penitentiary known as Parchman Farm, where Lewis and his fellow activists were humiliated, blasted by fire hoses with jets of water, and kept under inhumane conditions. On several of these occasions, he was beaten into an unconscious state. On other occasions, he was attacked by dogs.

Lewis's organization, the Student Nonviolent Coordinating Committee (SNCC), was a group of peace-loving freedom fighters, mostly young students, who would pray together the night before a protest, planned demonstration, or march. They also prepared for violence by role-playing for hours what they knew would await them in the angry, violent crowds that would attack them. They had to prepare because they knew this brutal treatment could occur at the hands of the police. Lewis recalled those preparations as he tried to describe the group's motivating force, what he called the spirit of history.

"We studied the whole idea of passive resistance. We were moved by the spirit of history," Lewis said in an interview.

We studied the way to love. That if someone beats you, or spits on you, or poured hot water or hot coffee on you, you looked straight ahead and nev-

Albemarle County, Virginia, 2019, near Charlottesville at sunset. This is the location of the lynching of John Henry James which occurred in 1918.

PHOTO: MICHAEL WILLIAMSON, WASHINGTON POST

er ever dreamed of hitting that person back or being violent toward that person. And we accepted it, most of us accepted it, as a way of life, as a way of living. This made us much better human beings. We had what we called role-playing or what some people would call social drama. Someone pretending that they were beating you or hitting you. And there were young people who would light a cigarette and then blow smoke in the faces of, in the eyes of, some of those people, preparing them for whatever could happen or might happen. We were shown how to curl our bodies so that our internal organs would escape direct blows. It was not enough to endure a beating. It was not enough to resist the urge to strike back at an assailant. That urge can't be there. You have to do more than just not hit back. You have to have no desire to hit back. You have to love that person who's hitting you. It was the most difficult of lessons. Hate is too heavy a burden to bear. If you start hating people, you must decide who you are going to hate tomorrow, who you are going to hate next week. Just love everybody. And

on one occasion I heard Dr. King say, "Just love the hell out of everybody. It's the better way. It's the best way."[21]

Finding purpose in pain has endured through three centuries in America. One area of our country known as sacred ground is in the deep southern states of Alabama, Mississippi, and Louisiana. During slavery, Mississippi and Alabama were referred to as "the coffin." Other southern states were where conductors on the Underground Railroad and other abolitionist organizations could plan secret escapes for enslaved Black people, but in the coffin, this was nearly impossible—or so it was thought. And during the 1960s' Freedom Summer bus trips across Tennessee, Alabama, and Mississippi, it was also found to be the most treacherous of the killing fields in the South.

Lewis said of the local conditions at the time, "Mississippi is now a bona fide police state. And the governor has a private army to suppress civil rights efforts." But the activists of the time believed, as Henry David Thoreau said, "Conscience should trump conformity."[22]

Sorrow Song

During the summer of 1964, buses filled with civil rights activists bravely drove across the states in the Deep South to protest segregation. All who signed on knew the danger and the importance of their campaign. They set out to defy an immoral law. The police sanctioned the separation of Black citizens to very inferior public spaces. In June 1964, three Freedom Summer workers—Michael Schwerner, Andrew Goodman, and James Chaney—disappeared in Neshoba County, Mississippi, after being jailed in Philadelphia.

The story of the search for Chaney, Schwerner, and Goodman is gruesome, but it also establishes the importance of memory and story as crucial features of any social justice struggle. During the search, the discovery of other Black bodies was a known fact for all who were involved with the movement at that time. It took two months to find the bodies of the murdered civil rights workers buried at a dam site in Neshoba County. In the first days and weeks after the men disappeared, Lewis joined the seemingly futile search for their bodies.[23]

> [We] walked around in the hot, sticky dusk, bugs buzzing around, out in the middle of nowhere, poking at scrub grass and bushes and dirt. It was really pretty useless, not to mention dangerous. . . . Rivers were dragged, woods were scoured, dirt was turned . . . and bodies were found. Old bodies, unidentified corpses, the decomposed remains of black people long given up as "missing." . . . It was ugly, sickening, horrifying. Here was proof—as if it was needed—that those woods and rivers in the heart of this state had long been a killing field, a dumping ground for the Klan.

The above quote is from the film *I Heard it Through the Grapevine*. In this documentary, there is an exchange between writer James Baldwin and David Dennis, Mississippi state coordinator of Congress of Racial Equality

Two community members fill soil jars at a commemoration ceremony.

PHOTO: EZE AMOS, C-VILLE WEEKLY

(CORE). Dennis was one of the leaders of Mississippi's Freedom Summer, a 1964 voter registration drive aimed at increasing the number of Black voters in Mississippi. Dennis narrates the scene in Philadelphia where Schwerner, Chaney, and Goodman were jailed. "We see their charred, burned-out car and the Neshoba County jail cell along with people searching for the bodies of the three civil rights workers," Dennis says. He recalls a gruesome revelation. While searching for the bodies of the missing civil rights workers, many other anonymous, abandoned dead bodies were found in the river.

> They found three bodies floating in the Mississippi one day. They had all been decapitated. Heads were gone. Cut up and everything else. Suddenly, it hits us: Black people buried under trees, floating in rivers, and everything else. People were being killed because they were attempting to get the right to vote.[24]

When faced with immense and horrific systemic violence such as this, the advice of elders is to take a shower, wear white, and go together into the darkness of such stories. When confronted with such inhumanity, we might feel temporarily blocked by the limit of our ability to endure. There may be anger that is unrestrained. For others, there is a broken spirit. Despite this, for change to happen, we have to share this horrendous, sorrowful story because we must get to where we empathize and care about the same things. Together, we must search for opportunities to resist injustice because discovering justice denied is the beginning of changing injustice. A society, and the people who live in it, won't evolve toward justice without hard work and detailed, true stories propelling that work forward—the work of the action steps and the emotional caretaking work.

These killing fields were sacred ground where authorities and White supremacist groups dumped unknown human beings with impunity under the cover of darkness. The dead were unidentified victims who were neither given burials nor identified and returned to their families. They were never memoried or storied. This truth may form yet another passionate choice point for change. The story has to be told. The story has to be shared with those who agree it happened and shared with those who deny it—because the story has to be changed.

Hope

Pushback

History teaches us that no matter what peace-loving social advocates do, violence will return. It is a good idea for organizers and advocates to anticipate negative pushback for any project, demonstration, or effort they are making on behalf of social justice. Injustice will persist, and hatred will live in our midst until we have found the fearful, troubled people capable of hate and violence and have answered their fear, ignorance, and ill will with appropriate consequences, education, dignity, and love. For those who act out and cause harm and those who refuse to change, we must live in a society where social norms and the law deliver consequences for hatred, violence, and racial terrorism. The pushback and negative resistance to social justice efforts can be celebrated as an invitation to address discrimination and to advance against it to heal and change. At the very least, it announces where the barriers to change are dwelling.

We will certainly continue to witness hate crimes and racial violence. This type of violence exists on a continuum of hatred and aggression. In its mildest and earliest form, racial violence may appear as ignorance, fear, verbal insults, and systemic discrimination. Today, we refer to some of these infractions as micro-aggressions. Without addressing such injustice, the behavior may grow and escalate into hate speech, dishonesty, or impulsiveness. After that, we frequently see threats, aggression, and widespread acceptance of injustice in policy or action, followed by actual, observable acts of violence which may escalate into

"Until we understand this history, understand this legacy, only then can we come together and really begin to **overcome** the racial distinctions that divide us."

—**Lonnie Bunch**, Smithsonian Secretary

Anti-lynching demonstrations by the NAACP challenged the American people and government to face the violence of lynching. In this 1934 photo, Howard University students stand with a symbolic noose hanging at their necks in a silent protest against ongoing murder, violence, and racial discrimination during the National Crime Conference in Washington, D. C., after the conference refused to discuss lynching as a national crime.

PHOTO: LIBRARY OF CONGRESS

Howard University students protest outside the National Crime Conference in Washington, DC, 1934. (© Bettmann/Getty Images.)

severe and persistent acts of destruction and war. Left unanswered, more minor acts of riot, ruination, and destruction escalate into terrorism or mass murder. Historians, scholars, journalists, and citizens identify examples of all these levels of violence against Black Americans currently and in past decades. Tragically, the stories and historical events have been numerous over the past 400 years.

Identifying acts of racial discrimination in the earliest stages on this continuum improves the possibility of a peaceful outcome. Before speech and behavior develop into aggression and violent acts, it is easier to intervene and be guided by the moral principle of human unity. One of the most important things we have in common is this: All of us are harmed by racial division and hate. All of us seek security and safety for our groups.

The public discussion of the four lynchings covered in these pages was mixed. The community remembrance projects shared in the stories in this book were not always welcomed by every member living in the communities involved. Coalition members in every locality were met with some pushback. It is important to anticipate such resistance and plan an answer for the negative responses. It's vital to see this as a milder form of discrimination and bias, which exists on a continuum.

As community remembrance projects enter the public space, the audience for the project may include some community members still denying the veracity of the events. This was true 140 years ago, and it is sadly still true today. The following inaccurate, dishonest reasons were given at the time of the lynchings of Charlotte Harris, John Henry James, Allie Thompson, and Frazier Baker:

1. Harris—The reason used to justify her lynching was that she was a bad employee who could not be trusted. They accused her of burning her employer's barn. The facts later established she did not burn the barn.

2. James—A mob accused him of raping a White woman. The woman's brother later confessed no rape had occurred.

3. Thompson—He was rumored to be having a consensual relationship with a White neighbor. Multiple relatives later admitted the woman was not involved with Allie at all and may have had dubious behavior and motives for being dishonest herself.

4. Baker—He refused to resign from a job he had been appointed to by the president of the United States. He had years of experience doing this job well in the neighboring Black community.

Today we know the facts: They were lynched for being Black. The murders stopped their free and hardworking lives. Lynching terrorized and threatened other Black citizens into submission.

Examples of pushback against a more accurate, inclusive narrative which survive to this day:

1. In the case of the lynching of Harris, which occurred in McGaheysville, Virginia, in 1878, a committee recently conducted planning to commemorate her and teach about what happened. Once this was made public in 2019, the descendant of the family who accused her of burning the barn wrote a lengthy letter to the Department of Historic Resources Board just weeks before the community remembrance project (CRP) was to take place, addressing the board: "I'm asking that you do NOT erect a monument to commemorate this woman. She was a very unpleasant woman and never got along well with her employer."[25] As hard as this erroneous pushback is to take, activists can engage

with it in order to refute it. In McGaheysville, Virginia, I am still working with other activists to engage in corrective conversations with White people clinging to historical amnesia, lost-cause mythology, and the lies told in the White family history version of the event. In this case, these conversations offer an opportunity to correct the record and locate where Harris is actually buried. Her burial site was one fact that came out of the conversations and research conducted for the CRP. Perhaps her descendants can be located. Now that her burial place is known, a soil conservation ceremony can take place. In the case of this lynching story, remembrance activities, racial healing, historical research, and hard conversations are ongoing as this book goes to press.

2. In the case of the lynching of Thompson in Culpeper, Virginia, community members planning the community remembrance ceremony were shocked and saddened when the local sheriff refused to attend. His opposition to acknowledging the crime and honoring Thompson was widely known.

3. In the CRP for James in Charlottesville, Virginia, the memorial committee was encouraged when historians and researchers were able to pinpoint with certainty where the lynching of James had occurred. This meant the soil collection and solemn memorial service would be in the actual location where the horrific event happened. The spot is near railroad tracks and a former blacksmith shop, now the site of a private golf and country club. Geologists and other experts used technology to locate the structure where the blacksmith shop used to stand. These landmarks are currently the location of a private golf and country club. When notified by area officials and CRP committee members that a sacred and meaningful soil collection ceremony was needed as a part of their lynching memorial activities, the board of directors at the country club slowed their cooperation and did not initially grant access. But this particular CRP committee represented several esteemed and credible sectors of the Charlottesville area, leaders from the academic, media, church, business, and economic communities. They let the club officials know how their non-cooperative position was about to play out in the ongoing press coverage, which was already considerably high profile. To their credit, the club reconsidered, and the ceremony moved forward despite the current landowners needing to be patiently encouraged to do the right thing.

4. In South Carolina, an honest history finally caught up to the moral outrage that occurred in 1898. Baker and his baby daughter, Julia, were murdered by a lynch mob when Baker refused to resign from his presi-

Equal Justice Initiative founder Bryan Stevenson stands with a Montgomery Slave Trade public marker. The forced migration of thousands of enslaved people from the upper South to the Deep South in the 19th century is a phenomenon most people don't understand. Recently erected markers are a part of a larger project to educate people about the legacy of slavery and the lasting effects that still exist in society today.

PHOTO: BOB MILLER, THE NEW YORK TIMES

dential-appointed job. In 2019, U.S. Representative Jim Clyburn joined the committee officials in a day of honor for the victims. If there was resistance, it did not show up in 2019. But that fact could not change the shameful story of the ill-fated trial years earlier. In 1898, after Baker was lynched, despite a fourteen-month investigation, the charges filed against the accused, and a two-week trial with national press coverage, an emissary from the attorney general's office in Washington, D.C., was dispatched as the trial came to a close, and the jury in the trial was unable to reach a verdict. The killers went free.

In the big picture, all of these racial justice advocates seeking to acknowledge one particular local lynching prevailed in their efforts. They succeeded in their plan to gather and say the names of the victims out loud. They honored their local victims of racial violence. They taught the true stories in the public space and demonstrated mercy, forgiveness, and a desire for reconciliation. The public campaigns to educate and raise awareness about systemic racism continue through their work and the work of others. Resistance did occur, and it always will, but in many of these cases, resistance was defeated. Violence did not have the last word; the cycle was interrupted.

It has been sixty-seven years since fourteen-year-old Emmett Till was lynched—for doing nothing—and in the seventy years since this boy was murdered, we have established a foundation, a memorial, and a place in our shared national memory for the story of his life and his death, but hate, threats, and violence have returned over and over. Every month, his Mississippi memorial is filled with bullet holes and splattered with paint. It is defaced with racial epithets, cracked, and broken under cover of night. Caretakers say this happens nearly every week. The hate and violence don't stop. It slows. It is contained. It is shaped and changed because consequences are delivered by social norms, laws, reporters, writers, photographers, vigilance, and social change. For some people, hate for and fear of a multiracial democracy for all citizens will never go away. So those who choose, like Ida B. Wells, to be ever vigilant have been weaving a timeless truth into the memory and the story of this period of our nation's history.

Currently, we are confronted with a severe case of historical amnesia and a horrendous whitewashing of the parts of our past marked by mob violence and racial terrorism. And at this consequential crossroads where Black history is attempting to be wiped white, there are some answers. Modern-day ac-

Participants listen and ask questions during a community education session regarding two lynchings which occurred in Frankfort, Kentucky.

tivists are responding to the people and groups who oppose freedom, equality, and safety for all. These are some of the questions they are answering:

Do those who hate freedom for all (especially people of color) think that collectively, as a people, activists are going to stop fighting for justice? *The fight for justice won't stop.* Do those who hate, fear, kill, and threaten innocent Black lives think that they can silence freedom-loving people? *They cannot silence freedom fighters.* Do they think a critical mass of Black freedom fighters, along with sympathetic White people, are going to stop speaking the truth? *Those advocates and their allies will not stop speaking their truth.* And to those who would plan to bend constitutional protections to preserve White-centered American institutions, do they believe that knowledge is going to take a vacation? *Because the scholars, activists, researchers, and other knowledge seekers did not cease their vigilance in the last 160 years. Again, in the current period of history, these teachers of truth will not take a vacation.*

The answers are quite clear. Collectively, as a people, there is a critical mass of activists who are not going to stop sharing about their lives and their experiences of oppression and harm. Not then and not now. That's not going to happen. Because change is on the march. The eternal answer is to tell the

A marble slab at the memorial contains the "Invocation:" *You will find us here memoried and storied.*

story. Tell it true. That is how a nation remembers without resorting to historical amnesia. And in time, a verified, documented, authentically true memory that's shared will be the universal story that endures. That can be the story of a new legacy of hope's triumph over human suffering.

Everyday Joy

Remembrance projects for the passing of Thompson, Harris, James, and Baker are symbolic projects at the beginning of a movement for remembrance and reparation in the larger culture. After the genealogical and historical research comes to a natural close, some answers may be provided. Perhaps descendants are located and receive the story of their distant relative and begin to speak openly about what they always knew to be true. Sometimes this happens for the very first time. As a remembrance project group agrees that we have probably found all that we can reasonably expect to find, the group's work begins to shift. They move into wanting to remember those ancestors lost to mass violence and racial terror: to honor them, apologize to them, and obtain accountability and visibility for them. It is not about a lynching now. It is about a funeral. And any funeral comes with the rituals of locating a meaningful place to remember, sharing thoughts and inspiring words, and celebrating the lives of those lost, those who remain, and those yet to come.

Even more important than the stories of their deaths and our remembrances of them are the stories and memories of the ordinary lives these people were living before they were captured and their loved ones and communities terrorized. Allie Thompson was captured and killed on a weekday from a field where he was working at his job. What else was happening in his life on that day? It's time to stop sharing only the pictures of the lynching tree. I hesitate to even use the words that bring these pictures to mind. But I do so in the spirit of a sacred reverence that the heroes of any war or struggle deserve. The dangling feet. The limp bodies. The long shot of the bridge and the crowds salaciously gathered around the spectacle. Others have written of the dual purpose of the violence. A message was meant to be sent to the Black community to return to a different type of enslavement. It was sent.

Now, it's long past time to change the narrative and imagine the simple joys that marked these people's lives—like the church dinners, school class-

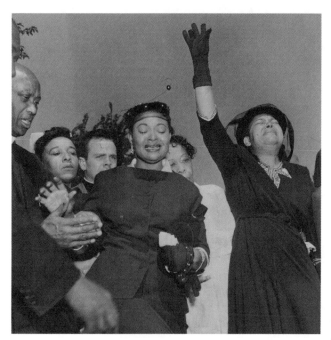

When her son was brutally beaten, tortured, and killed in Mississippi in 1955, Mamie Till courageously decided to release the photographs of his mutilated corpse and allow public coverage of his funeral in order to tell the truth of his death at the hands of White supremacists.

PHOTO: LIBRARY OF CONGRESS

rooms, the weddings, and the baptisms. One such imagined scene is depicted on the cover of this book in the Ment Nelson painting, *A Backwoods Baptism*. It is time to ask: Where are the family gatherings, the homegoings, the stories of enlistments, the vacations, the engagements, and the parties? All families keep these stories. Families nurture each other's souls and survive unthinkable horrors on the memories, nurturance, and sense of belonging from these stories. Why doesn't the entirety of our current U.S. culture clamor to weave these survival stories into our shared narrative of U.S. history? To learn from the brave stories of surviving terror and becoming resilient. To tell the truth about the horrific violence, cover-up, and historical amnesia that followed is the point of this book. Hopefully, our knowledge and telling of history can evolve to locate Black Americans in a rightful place in our national memory of everyday joys, everyday struggles, and everyday triumphs. Our country deserves better. America deserves to celebrate a shared history of the honest truth, including the mistakes and what was done to reconcile and account for errors. This is the way to a secure and peaceful life for all.

Invocation

Within the story of American racial violence is an open question: Will the title of the next chapter in our shared history be "Love Wins"? Or, as many public commentators today believe, are we all living in a chapter named "We are slowly destroying each other"? This struggle is not about who will win. It is about love—a type of love that comes from cohesion. As a national family living in community, we may share the commitment to getting the public history right.

American writer Elizabeth Alexander's poem, "Invocation," is displayed prominently in a sculpture at the National Monument for Peace and Justice in Montgomery, Alabama. In it, she implores all of those who visit to remember and call each name of those lynched. In that way, those injured or killed by such violence will remain in memory. Here, they will remain in story.

In sharing these memories of survival and trauma, we make the story of our collective history and healing more accurate and robust. Learning this shared history makes it possible to see clear crossroads and potential turning points behind us on the path. By remaining aware of these choice points in our current struggle to deliver a more just society, we can respond honorably to the ancestors' call.

Conclusion

In the history books and in my real life, the many empathetic racial justice warriors I've worked with and read about teach me to ask and answer these key questions about race in America. I do this for myself, and I come from the context and limits of my own lived experience.

As a White person, what unearned advantages do I receive as a result of being White?

How can I use my unearned advantage to weaken systems of unearned advantage?

Why would I want to?

Why do matters of race matter so much, and why do I care?

This book is my answer to these and other questions. I am White, and yet this book is about racial violence and racial terrorism toward Black Americans. Because I am White in America, the automatically assumed treatment I receive from police includes safety and protection. Black Americans cannot assume the same. All of the activists I read and write about know this is a fact because it is present in research statistics and documentation across numerous social institutions such as the criminal justice system, the legal system, the financial system, education, health care, housing, lending, banking, and employment. I know it, too. These are indisputable facts.

While attempting to bring the two themes of racial violence and personal trauma to the page, many fields of educational knowledge helped me in my quest to understand the how and the why of the racial hatred that persists in America today. Interdisciplinary history, where investigators such as cultural anthropologists and developmental psychologists

By the 1830s, the domestic slave trade was integral to the economy and the businesses of the South. Black men, women, and children were sold in droves and ordered to march in chains from Staunton, Virginia, to Tennessee. The artist writes on this watercolor, "I was astonished at this boldness. The carrier stopped, and then ordered the march." Scholars believe that lynching was a type of bias-motivated terrorism that sought to return society to the level of domination and control known during slavery.

PHOTO: LIBRARY OF CONGRESS

pick up the mission of historical research and use social science tools to answer different—but related—questions, has advanced our scholarship and our activism. Another helpful theory is the ecological systems theory of human development advanced by Urie Bronfenbrenner and others. This developmental theory shines a light on how the context of our historical times affects individuals, families, and communities for good and for bad. Both can be applied to advance the teaching and learning of Black history. These disciplines of scholarship compelled me to ask why racial hatred and violence persist and to write down the answers I have learned.

In the process of that learning, it slowly became apparent to me why it is crucial to center ourselves in our own limitations and to share these limits as we connect with people and groups fighting for racial justice. The point is this: Without acknowledging personal suffering and vulnerability, deep, authentic empathy for others remains stilted, if not impossible. If a person who has been harmed or has perpetrated harm stays in denial, the effect of the denied hurt feelings can be the engine that drives the projection of one's faults onto "the other." Instead of uncovering truth, those in denial participate in blame and target anyone other than themselves. Feeling the feelings cannot be tolerated. Projection and delusion are necessary defense mechanisms against the feelings which come with acknowledging hard truth. This aggressive deadlock against progress may remain the status quo until trusting, authentic empathetic relationships invite those who care into a process where we can recognize the truth, share what happened, share the feelings, and begin to heal. I have participated in this process personally. I have watched hundreds of my patients and their families experience this progression and healing. And I am certain the same concepts can inform our current struggles in groups and as a nation.

My experience informs the work I do and the stories I tell. I know how a lack of accountability can compound the suffering endured by the victims of harm. I have felt the pain of the invisible one.

I wrote this book and share these stories because of my personal dedication and allyship in activism for racial equality. My professional experience and work history contains teaching, research, and writing in the area of eradicating racial harm to effect improvement in the sociocultural contexts of human development. This is what I know for sure. None of us develops in a vacuum. All individuals living in our culture during these historical times will continue to be negatively affected by our failure to address discrimination in the system because discrimination's harmful effects do not simply cause harm for the individual; discrimination harms everyone. A systems-based understanding of human development can also guide targeted interventions for change and prevention of harm and trauma before they begin. The result of increased systemic justice and improved accountability for the harms of racial injustice is an improved adjustment for all people living in those systems.

I do not believe that my experience as a victim of trauma, alcoholism, family violence, and loss qualifies me to make a personal comparison to the trauma of racial violence or racialized trauma. As a White person living in my culture at this time in history, I have not experienced racial discrimination or trauma. But for the reasons I've listed below, I believe certain aspects of the healing process are the same.

1. All stories of suffering have the potential to help others, even if the specific nature of that suffering is very, very different and not comparable.

2. I know firsthand that empathy and listening can save lives and unlock bitter and hate-filled hearts because that happened for me. This is something I only learned during the recovery process.

3. I was a victim. But victims become witnesses, and witnesses become survivors. And survivors are resilient.

4. The experience of victimhood often occurs in multiple contexts because being harmed and abused makes an individual vulnerable to perpetrators of harm. In my case, after the unacknowledged, unhealed trauma of childhood separation from my birth parents, I was a victim in four other contexts before I began to get honest and receive help. Again, this is something I never knew until I was in treatment for trauma. The learning is a part of the healing.

5. When victims get help and recover, they may have a sixth sense and a "been there/felt that" intuition that may help another person get the help they need. It helped me to speak with someone else who had experienced the same thing or something similar to my experience.

6. When a victim regains their balance, it is the job of survivors, if they choose, to contribute to the healing of others through the process of sharing

The author paying respects in McGaheysville, Virginia, at the probable gravesite of Charlotte Harris on March 6, 2022, the 144th anniversary of her death.

A mourner is overcome with emotion near the site of the blacksmith shop where the Charlottesville lynching occurred.

PHOTO: MICHAEL WILLIAMSON, WASHINGTON POST

their story and offering a path to healing. It is a crucial aspect of recovery from trauma. The suffering comes to have a purpose of sorts.

The lynching stories profiled in this book contain the deeply personal family stories of descendants who are living today. In some cases, these descendants need community cohesion and the help of others to complete their stories and heal. Collectively, as a people, when we tell the truth in our public history, learning these stories and participating in the remembrance becomes a part of our own healing as well.

Acknowledgements

This book began in an instant. Two women were there at the start.

To Sharyn Pinney, a freedom fighter and an excellent civil rights study trip partner, I want to thank you for being my outgoing and overly social soul sister forever and my adventurous partner in all things.

Sister Evelyn Craig is the spiritual warrior who first helped me see the plan. With her prayerful and humble presence, Sister Evie discerns God's path for me and many others. She led me to listen to the ghosts in Montgomery. I hope I have told their stories and that, God willing, I will have the opportunity to continue to do so.

It is my belief that our history of racism is a shared history. I am deeply indebted to the people I've met in my life who share their history with me. Only through these personal encounters can we identify what we are individually responsible for in the healing process. Most of all, I am grateful for the trust and intimacy we shared as we grapple with feelings and make plans to stay in the fight for equality. None of us absorb the horrors of lingering systemic racism or make personal change a priority without friends who know us well, challenging us to do better, loving us as we try. Thank you, Khadijah Islam, Marysue Wheeler, Esther Nizer, Shayne Bullen, Nancy Harrold, Janie Watson, and Elaine Blakey, for trusting me with your friendship and being faithful co-conspirators for good trouble. As an added side benefit, the self-doubt and fear that comes with writing anything was taken care of from the beginning by making a call to these sister-friends who are now fellow matriarchs and have my back in all things.

Many of the courthouse discoveries for the Charlotte Harris case were made possible by the work of Zann Nelson. Creative and relentless Zann, who always buries the gold until it's "time" but never fails to deliver new facts in any phone conversation about genealogy casework or community organizing.

There are far more Reconcilers than Haters in our country. To nurture each other, to continue to speak up and prove it, we need to read, write, and publish more accurate and inclusive Black history. These talented women helped me write, edit, research, publicize, publish and polish this book in a way that I hope is sensitive, inspirational, knowledgeable, and accurate. To Jae Hermann, Tia Ross, Caite Hamilton, Ann Weinstock, Teri Rider, Chelsea Robinson, Kayla Kauffman, Chandra Gore, and Dawn Michelle Hardy, a mere thank you is not enough. Please know how valuable you are in teaching the craft of writing and the profession of publishing, for nurturing those you work with, and for inspiring storytellers everywhere.

In 2021, I heard historian Nell Painter say, "If you want to write a book, you have to leave home." Thank you, Dr. Painter, for realistic expectations, depth of knowledge, academic analysis, and suggesting a method to finish the writing.

Trudy Hale is the caretaker extraordinaire of Porches Writing Retreat, a writing community and residence in Norwood, VA, where I was able to leave home but stay near home and create this work in the company of other writers. Thank you for your hospitality and encouragement, Trudy.

Since the beginning of this project, my mission has been to connect people to other people who care about ending racial discrimination, harm, and violence. No one cares more than the talented activists and teachers who helped me stay the course. In addition, it is the privilege of my life to share a mission with such gifted community organizers. Together I hope we may continue to teach people what they can do to live a more multi-racialized life where we care about all our neighbors and amplify an accurate and inclusive Black history in our communities. Thank you, Monica Robinson, Gianluca De Fazio, Karen Thomas, Jalane Schmidt, and Steven Thomas.

Last but truly, always first, I am grateful to my husband and our family, who believe in me and love me always. Thank you, Bob, Will, Julia, Emily, Kelle, Ben, and Chris. In our family, we work to respect and improve our children's legacy. This book was written for all of America's children, who will live with our progress and our mistakes. I would like to say to my grandchildren—Lydia, August, Leo, Eli, Emma, Mae, Walter, and Belle—it is for you that I try every day to take action to admit and amend the mistakes we have made. In you, I feel the urgency and the hope for change. You inspire me to tell a true story and to stay committed to never going back to the silence America has held up for far too long about racial harms. Because of you, I believe that it is not too late to rebuild our multi-racial democracy in a truly merciful, just, and visible way.

Endnotes

One | Story

1   killed for breaking a social rule. *True Justice: Bryan Stevenson's Fight for Equality*, distributed by HBO, produced and directed by Peter Kunhardt, Teddy Kunhardt, and George Kunhardt, June, 2019, https://www.kunhardtfilmfoundation.org/film-archive/true-justice.

Two | Acknowledgment

2   throughout Virginia during these years. Gianluca De Fazio, Racial Terror: Lynching in Virginia, 1877-1927, James Madison University, https://www.jmu.edu/africana/racial-terror.shtml.

3   in a civilized community. Gianluca De Fazio, Racial Terror: Lynching in Virginia, 1877-1927, James Madison University, "A Virginia Atrocity-Disguised Men Hang a Woman to a Sapling," March 11, 1878, Washington Evening Star, https://sites.lib.jmu./valynchings/va1878030601.

4   none of them have been arrested. Chronicling America, Library of Congress, "Barbarism in Virginia: An Innocent Woman Cruelly Hanged by Masked Men," Evening Star 1854-1972, April 17, 1878, https://chronicalingamerica.loc.gov.

5   **live together as brothers.** Martin L. King, Jr., address delivered at the Fourth Constitutional Convention of the American Federation of Labor and Congress of Industrial Organizations (AFL-CIO), Miami Beach, FL, December 11, 1961, speech may be found in: Michael K. Honey, All Labor Has Dignity, Boston: Beacon Press, 2012.

6   **where the wound was made.** Alice Walker, *The Way Forward is With a Broken Heart*, (London: Phoenix, 2005).

Three | Remembrance

7   **three miles from Culpeper.** Chronicling America, Library of Congress, "Mob Overpowers Jailors and Hangs Negro to Tree," *Richmond Times-Dispatch*, Richmond, Va, November 30, 1918, https://chroniclingamerica.loc.gov/lccn/ sn83045389/1918-11-30/ed-1/seq-3/.

8   **at the hands of unknown persons.** Zann Nelson and Allison Brophy Champion, "The Untold Story of Allie Thompson," *Culpeper Star-Exponent*, January 15, 2006.

9   **why we need to learn about it,** Jeff Say, "Raising Awareness of Lynching in Culpeper," Inside Nova, August 16, 2018, accessed April 28, 2022, https:// www.insidenova.com/culpeper/raising-awareness-of-lynching-in-culpeper/article_ a0eede16-a15e-11e8-877f-7b0f5abca95e.html.

Four | Healing

10   **home on Monday morning.** Chronicling America, Library of Congress, "A Dastardly Crime," *Staunton Spectator and Vindicator*, Staunton, Va., July 14, 1898, https://chroniclingamerica.loc.gov/lccn/sn84024720/1898-07-14/ed-1/seq-3/.

11   **ice cream in the park.** Norah Mulinda, "Historical Marker Unveiled for Lynching Victim John Henry James," Charlottesville Tomorrow, July 15, 2019, https://www.cvilletomorrow.org/articles/historical-marker-unveiled-for-lynching-victim-john-henry-james/.

12   **of Hotopp's assailant.** Chronicling America, Library of Congress, "A

Negro Lynched in Albemarle," *The Times*, Richmond, Va. July 13, 1898, https://chroniclingamerica.loc.gov/lccn/sn85034438/1898-07-13/ed-1/seq-1/.

13 **accomplish his foul purpose.** Chronicling America, Library of Congress, "John James Hanged: The Negro Assailant of Miss Hotopp Met by a Mob," *Shenandoah Herald*, Woodstock, Va., July 15, 1898, https://chroniclingamerica.loc.gov/lccn/sn85026941/1898-07-15/ed-1/seq-2/.

14 **the Newport News Daily.** Uncommonwealth Virginia Memory.com. "Judge Lynch at Work," *Newport News Daily Press*, Virginia, July 13, 1898, The Legacy of John Henry James - The UncommonWealth, https://uncommonwealth.virginiamemory.com/blog/2018/06/06/the-legacy-of-john-henry-james/.

15 **the White woman, Hotopp.** Chronicling America, Library of Congress, "A Dastardly Crime," Staunton Spectator and Vindicator, Staunton, Va., July 14, 1898, https://chroniclingamerica.loc.gov/lccn/sn84024720/1898-07-14/ed-1/seq-3/.

16 **terrible ordeal of a public trial.** Chronicling America, Library of Congress, "A Dastardly Crime," Staunton Spectator and Vindicator, Staunton, Va., July 14, 1898, https://chroniclingamerica.loc.gov/lccn/sn84024720/1898-07-14/ed-1/seq-3/.

17 **persons unknown to the jury.** Chronicling America, Library of Congress, "A Brutal Murder-Mob Makes No Efforts at Disguise," *Richmond Planet*, July 16, 1898, https://chroniclingamerica.loc.gov.

Five | Change

18 **die running as standing still!** Nicole Lovely Park, "Lynching of Frazier and Julia B Baker," Build Nation (blog), November 10, 2015, https://buildnationblog.wordpress.com/2015/11/10/lynching-of-julia-and-frazier-b-baker/.

19 **to serve in a position of authority.** Trichita M. Chestnut, prologue, *Lynching: Ida B. Wells-Barnett and the Outrage over the Frazier Baker Murder*, (Fall 2008), p. 23, https://www.archives.gov/files/publications/prologue/2008/fall/lynching.pdf.

20 **the watchword of freedom.** Ida B. Wells, *The Autobiography of Ida B. Wells*, 2nd ed. (Chicago: University of Chicago Press, 2020), 390.

Six | Memory

21   It's the best way. Jon Meacham, *His Truth is Marching On*, (New York: Random House, 2020), 58.

22   Conscience should trump conformity. Jon Meacham, *His Truth is Marching On*, 59.

23   futile search for their bodies. Jon Meacham, *His Truth is Marching On*, 159.

24   to get the right to vote. Eddie Glaude, *Begin Again: James Baldwin's America and Its Urgent Lessons for Our Own*, (New York: Crown, 2020), 159.

Seven | Hope

25   got along well with her employer. Personal letter from John H. Sipes to the Virginia Department of Historic Resources Board, Richmond, Va., June 18, 2020, https://www.dhr.virginia.gov/wp-content/uploads/2020/06/John-H-Sipe-statement.pdf.

Bibliography

Bailey, Amy Kate, and Stewart Tolnay. *Lynched: The Victims of Southern Mob Violence*. Chapel Hill: The University of North Carolina Press, 2015.

Baptist, Edward. *The Half has Never Been Told: Slavery and The Making of American Capitalism*. New York: Basic Books, 2014.

Carr, Cynthia. *Our Town: A Heartland Lynching, a Haunted Town, and the Hidden History of White America*. New York: Three Rivers Press, 2007.

Carter, David. "Outraged Justice: The Lynching of Postmaster Frazier Baker in Lake City, South Carolina, 1897-1899." Undergraduate Thesis, University of North Carolina at Chapel Hill, 1992.

Chesnutt, Trichita. Prologue to *Lynching: Ida B. Wells-Barnett and the Outrage over the Frazier Baker Murder*. Fall, 2008.

Delea, Pete. "City, County to Dedicate Charlotte Harris Marker." *Harrisonburg Daily News-Record*, September 24, 2020. https://www.dnronline.com/dnronline/city-county-to-dedicate-charlotte-harris-marker/article_5e2ad069-c166-52f1-8413-da1cbde02ed7.html.

DeWolf, Thomas, and Jodie Geddes. *The Little Book of Racial Healing*. New York: Good Books, 2019.

DeWolf, Thomas, and Sharon Leslie Morgan. *Gathering at the Table: The Healing Journey of a Daughter of Slavery and a Son of the Slave Trade.* Boston: Beacon Press, 2012.

DuRocher, Kristina. *Raising Racists: The Socialization of White Children in the Jim Crow South*. Lexington: The University Press of Kentucky, 2011.

Duster, Michelle. *Ida B. the Queen: The Extraordinary Life and Legacy of Ida B. Wells*. New York: One Signal Atria, 2021.

Equal Justice Initiative (website). "Living Legacy: Voices From Lynching in America—Confronting the Legacy of Racial Terror." Accessed May 28, 2022. https://lynchinginamerica.eji.org.

Ford, Dionne, and Jill Strauss, eds. *Slavery's Descendants: Shared Legacies of Race & Reconciliation*. New Brunswick: Rutgers University Press, 2019.

Giddings, Paula. *Ida: A Sword Among Lions: Ida B. Wells and the Campaign Against Lynching*. New York: Amistad, 2008.

Glaude, Eddie. *Begin Again: James Baldwin's America and Its Urgent Lessons for Our Own*. New York: Crown, 2020.

Hannah-Jones, Nikole, Caitlin Roper, Ilena Silverman, and Jake Silverstein, eds. *The 1619 Project: A New American Origin Story*. London: Random House, 2021.

Helms, Joe. "Sacred Ground, Now Reclaimed." *Washington Post*, July 7, 2018.

Holman-Conwill, Kinshasha, and Paul Gardullo, eds. *Make Good the Promises: Reclaiming Reconstruction and Its Legacies*. New York: Amistad, 2021.

Hubl, Thomas. *Healing Collective Trauma: A Process for Integrating Our Intergenerational and Cultural Wounds*. Boulder: Sounds True, 2020.

Ifill, Sherrilyn A. *On the Courthouse Lawn: Confronting the Legacy of Lynching in the 21st Century*. Boston: Beacon Press, 2007.

Jeffers, Honoree Fanonne. *The Love Songs of W.E.B. Dubois*. New York: HarperCollins, 2021.

Johnson, Krista. "1898 Charlottesville Lynching Victim Joins Those Honored at EJI." *Montgomery Advertiser*, July 12, 2018.

Kendi, Ibram X., and Blain Keisha, eds. *Four Hundred Souls: A Community History of African America: 1619-2019*. New York: One World, 2021.

Kendi, Ibram X. *How to be An Antiracist*. New York: Random House, 2019.

Kilby, Phoebe, and Betty Kilby-Baldwin. *Cousins: Connected Through Slavery, a Black Woman and a White Woman Discover Their Past—and Each Other*.

Lancaster: Walnut Street Books, 2021.

King, Ruth. *Mindful of Race: Transforming Racism from the Inside Out.* Boulder: Sounds True, 2018.

Kytle, Ethan J., and Blain Roberts. *Denmark Vesey's Garden: Slavery and Memory in the Cradle of the Confederacy.* New York: The New Press, 2018.

Lancaster, Guy. *American Atrocity.* Fayetteville: The University of Arkansas Press, 2021.

Markovitz, Jonathan. *Legacies of Lynching: Racial Violence and Memory.* Minneapolis: University of Minnesota Press, 2004.

Marsh, Charles. *The Beloved Community: How Faith Shapes Social Justice, from The Civil Rights Movement to Today.* New York: Basic Books, 2005.

McGhee, Heather. *The Sum of Us: What Racism Costs Everyone and How We Can Prosper Together.* New York: One World, 2021.

Meacham, Jon. *His Truth is Marching On: John Lewis and The Power of Hope.* New York: Random House, 2020.

Meacham, Jon. *The Soul of America: The Battle for Our Better Angels.* New York: Random House, 2018.

Meeks, Catherine, and Nibs Stroupe. *Passionate for Justice: Ida B. Wells as Prophet for Our Time.* New York: Church Publishing, Inc., 2019.

Miles, Tiya. *All That She Carried: The Journey of Ashley's Sack, a Black Family Keepsake.* New York: Random House, 2021.

Mulinda, Norah. "Historical Marker Unveiled for Lynching Victim John Henry James." *Charlottesville Tomorrow*, July 15, 2019. https://www.cvilletomorrow.org/articles/historical-marker-unveiled-for-lynching-victim-john-henry-james/.

Nelson, Zann, and Allison Brophy Champion. "The Untold Story of Allie Thompson." *Culpeper Star Exponent*, January 15, 2006.

Pennington, James W. C. *A Narrative of Events of the Life of J.H. Banks, An Escaped Slave, From the Cotton State of Alabama.* Scott's Valley: CreateSpace Independent Publishing, 2018.

Provence, Lisa. "Complicit: Pilgrimage Acknowledges Charlottesville Legacy of Lynching." *C-VILLE Weekly*, May 16, 2018. https://www.c-ville.com/complicit-pilgrimage-acknowledges-charlottesvilles-legacy-lynching/.

Singh, Anneliese. *The Racial Healing Handbook: Practical Activities to Help You Challenge Privilege, Confront Systemic Racism & Engage in Collective Healing.* Oakland: New Harbinger, 2019.

Smith, Clint. *How the Word is Passed.* New York: Little, Brown and Company, 2021.

Stevenson, Bryan. *Just Mercy.* New York: Random House, 2014.

Tripp, Mike. "New Historical Marker on Court Square Tells Story of Charlotte Harris' Lynching." *The Citizen*, September 28, 2020. https://hburgcitizen.com/2020/09/28/new-historical-marker-on-court-square-tells-story-of-charlotte-harris-lynching/.

Wetzler, Jessica. "Locals Talk Lynching History." *Harrisonburg Daily News-Record*, September 17, 2019. https://www.dnronline.com/news/local/locals-talk-lynching-history/article_ca8fd651-8238-53e1-8188-7ac7333e1e6b.html.

Wexler, Laura. *Fire in A Canebrake: The Last Mass Lynching in America.* New York: Scribner, 2003.

Wilkerson, Isabel. *Caste: The Origins of Our Discontents.* New York: Random House, 2020.

Williams, Chad, Kidada Williams and Keisha Blain, eds. *The Charleston Syllabus: Readings on Race, Racism and Racial Violence.* Athens: The University of Georgia Press, 2016.

Williams, Kidada. *They Left Great Marks on Me: African American Testimonies of Racial Violence from Emancipation to World War I.* New York: New York University Press, 2012.

To Learn More About Healing Racial Violence

Commemoration Activism and Expanding Public History

The Jefferson School African American Heritage Center
www.jeffschoolheritagecenter.org

Maryland Lynching Memorial Project
www.mdlynchingmemorial.org

NMAACH National Museum of African American History & Culture
www.nmaahc.si.edu

Shenandoah Valley Black Heritage Project
www.valleyblackheritage.org

Coming to The Table
www.comingtothetable.org

Southern Poverty Law Center Podcast: "Learning for Justice"
(formerly "Teaching Tolerance")
www.splcenter.org

African American Intellectual History Society (AAIHS)
www.aaihs.org

Encyclopedia Virginia
www.virginiahumanities.org

Arkansas Peace and Justice Memorial Movement
www.apjmm.org

MLK Workgroup on Lynchings in Virginia
http://mklcommission.dls.virginia.gov/lynchinginvirginia.html

EJI Community Remembrance Projects
https://eji.org/projects/community-remembrance-project/

NAACP
www.naacp.org

Racial Terror: Lynching in Virginia, 1877-1927 Research Project
https://sites.lib.jmu.edu/valynchings/

Antiracist Education and Training

CSWAC – The Center for The Study of White American Culture, Inc.
www.cswac.org
Each workshop is conducted by a team of CSWAC facilitators who are also racial justice activists with a history as organizers working in cross-racial alliances.

Coming To The Table
www.comingtothetable.org
Community groups meet monthly throughout the U.S.. Their mission is to confront the legacy of slavery to reclaim a more complete picture of U.S. history, one cousin at a time.

Patti Digh, Hard Conversations Book Club
www.pattidigh.com

Truth Racial Healing and Transformation projects
www.healourcommunities.org
The W. K. Kellogg Foundation supports local communities as they build coalitions for seeking change to end racial oppression, racial harms and discrimination. TRHT is a national effort with transformation projects in over 14 communities such as www.blackbeltfound.org. in Selma Alabama. Learn more at: www.everychildthrives.com.

Center for Justice and Peacebuilding at Eastern Mennonite University
www.emu.edu/cjp/about

Mindful of Race Institute – Online Learning Academy
www.mindfulofraceinstitute.teachable.com *and* www.ruthking.net

The Mindful of Race Institute was established to support individuals seeking to engage in the inner work of racial healing and social intimacy. Their educational programs provide an introspective investigation of our racial conditioning and impact.

Absalom Jones Center for Racial Healing
www.centerforracialhealing.org

The mission of this Episcopal center for racial healing is to provide tools and experiences that allow faith communities, and the larger community of individuals, to engage in dismantling racism through education, prayer, dialogue, pilgrimage, and spiritual formation.

Image Credits

p. x. Library of Congress. NAACP headquarters flies a flag announcing a lynching.

p. xii. Author's photo. The Memorial for Peace and Justice in Montgomery, Alabama.

p. 3. Author's photo. The sculpture "Raise Up" by Hank Willis Thomas is displayed at the Memorial in Montgomery.

p. 4. Author's photo. A visit to EJI's National Monument for Peace and Justice Memorial exposes the history of White Supremacy.

p. 6. Photo by Eze Amos/C-VILLE Weekly. Inside the Legacy Museum, hundreds of jars of soil from commemoration ceremonies are displayed.

p. 9. Author's photo. The Charlotte Harris Historical Marker in Harrisonburg, Virginia.

p. 10. Photo by Mike Tripp/The Harrisonburg Citizen. Charlotte Harris is commemorated in Harrisonburg, Virginia.

p. 13. Author's photo. Charlotte Harris's body remained hanging on this country road for three days.

p. 14. Author's photo. Wreath laying at graveside "Beloved Slaves Ceremony" in Elkton, Virginia.

p. 18. Author's photo. The Allie Thompson historical marker located at the National Monument for Peace and Justice in Montgomery, Alabama.

p. 20. Photo by Allison Brophy Champion/Culpeper Star Exponent. Culpeper community members gather to commemorate the life and death of Allie Thompson.

p. 22. Photo by Michael Williamson/Washington Post/Getty Images. Soil collection at the John Henry James lynching site.

p. 25. Photo by Eze Amos/Charlottesville Tomorrow. Community members gather in Charlottesville.

p. 26. Photo by Michael Williamson/Washington Post/Getty Images. Dr. Brenda Brown-Grooms listens deeply to remarks at the Charlottesville memorial.

p. 29. Author's photo. A marker hangs at the EJI memorial in Montgomery, Alabama, to acknowledge John Henry James publicly.

p. 30. Photo by Julie Bennett/USA Today Network. A Charlottesville community member adds soil in a ceremony conducted in Alabama.

p. 33. Library of Congress. Frazier Baker's widow and surviving children.

p. 34. Photo by Donna Tracy/SCNOW/The Morning News, Florence, S.C./Lee Enterprises. A historical marker is erected at the site where Frazier Baker and his family were attacked in 1898.

p. 37. Photo by Donna Tracy/SCNOW/The Morning News, Florence, S.C/Lee Enterprises. Dr. Fostenia Baker participates in a Remembrance Ceremony for her uncle, Frazier Baker.

p. 38. Library of Congress. Journalist, activist, and teacher Ida Wells pictured with her four children.

p. 41. Photo by Donna Tracy/SCNOW/The Morning News, Florence, S.C/Lee Enterprises. A marker is displayed in Lake City, South Carolina, near the lynching of U.S. Postmaster Frazier Baker.

p. 45. The Belleville News Democrat, Belleville, Illinois. A protest sign seen at an anti-racist demonstration.

p. 47. Author's photo. A sculpture by artist Kwame Akoto-Bamfo stands at the National Monument for Peace and Justice in Montgomery, Alabama.

p. 48. Library of Congress. Slave traders' office of Price and Birch, located in Alexandria, Virginia.

p. 51. Photo by Michael Williamson/Washington Post/Getty Images. Location of the lynching of John Henry James.

p. 52. Photo by Eze Amos/C-VILLE Weekly. Two community members fill a soil jar at the lynching site in Charlottesville, Virginia.

p. 56. Library of Congress. In 1934, Howard University students and other NAACP members performed an anti-lynching demonstration.

p. 59. Photo by Bob Miller/The New York Times/Redux. Equal Justice Initiative Bryan Stevenson stands with a Montgomery Slave Trade public marker.

p. 61. Photo credit The State Journal, Frankfort, Kentucky. Participants at a memorial point their fingers to the sky to remember those lost to racial violence. The ceremony memorialized two African Americans lynched in Frankfort, Kentucky.

p. 62. Author's photo. A marble slab at the National Memorial for Peace and Justice contains the Elizabeth Alexander poem, Invocation. *"You will find us here memoried and storied."*

p. 64. Library of Congress. Mamie Till, the mother of lynching victim Emmett Till, seen here at her son's funeral.

p. 67. Library of Congress; In the 1830s, Black men, women and children were sold in droves and marched from Virginia to Tennessee and the Deep South.

p. 68. Author photo. Paying respect in McGaheysville, Virginia, at the gravesite of lynching victim Charlotte Harris.

p. 70. Photo by Michael Williamson/Washington Post/Getty Images; A mourner is overcome with emotion at the Charlottesville commemoration ceremony.

Back cover. Photo by Anne McQuary/The New York Times. On Saturday, July 26, 2008, Author Toni Morrison, far left, leads the procession during a ceremony dedicating her "bench by the road."

Index

Dr. Judith Reifsteck

Since 1976, Dr. Judith Reifsteck has worked as a writer, licensed professional counselor, university professor, social science researcher, and psychotherapist. In 2016, she took a break from teaching and psychotherapy to write full time. Dr. Reifsteck is a mother, grandmother and community volunteer for racial justice coalitions. She writes narrative non-fiction, editorials, and essays.

During her work as an individual and family counselor for 40 years, Dr. Reifsteck worked with trauma victims, refugees, and those in recovery. She also taught and conducted research from a systemic perspective. In the college class-room she taught Lifespan Human Development, Abnormal Psychology, and Trauma Healing and Reconciliation.

The purpose of her writing is *to advocate for the vulnerable who do not have visibility or a voice in their communities*. She hopes her work leads others to join together in multiracial coalitions to learn an accurate and inclusive Black His-tory. She believes that in memorializing the stories and the victims of racial injustice, we may repair the trauma and tell the true story of structural racism in America.